ADVANCED ENGLISH SERIES

Grammar & Diagramming Sentences

by Gianni DeVincentis-Hayes, Ph.D

Book cover design by Kathy Kifer

To my husband, Jimmy, and my daughters, Marta and Brynne:
Thanks for always being there for me, for helping when I'm so
busy, and for understanding.

A special word of gratitude goes to Polly Stewart, Ph.D, in
English linguistics; professor emeritus of Salisbury University,
for all her proofreading input.

Copyright © 1995 Stanley H. Collins
Revised 2006

Published by
Garlic Press
605 Powers St.
Eugene, OR 97402

ISBN 978-0-9319-9375-6
Reorder Number GP-075
Printed in China

www.garlicpress.com

Table of Contents

Introduction

Grammar and Diagramming Sentences focuses on teaching the basics of diagramming by taking students step-by-step through the process, presenting simple concepts initially, and then building on those concepts until the student feels comfortable diagramming detailed compound-complex constructions. This systematic approach is not only easy for students to grasp, but it also helps build their confidence in learning a grammar technique that isn't frequently taught in schools today.

A **diagnostic exam** at the beginning of the text allows students to determine their aptitude for diagramming.

Each **chapter** opens with a brief introduction of the major topics to be covered, followed by straightforward, easy-to-understand examples and illustrations. Each chapter provides ample opportunity for practice with activities involving 40-60 problems. And finally, each chapter includes a review summarizing the key points and major rules presented.

Sequential **review tests** occur after every two chapters. Although these tests cover in detail the two previous chapters, they also reassess skills from all preceding chapters.

A **mastery exam** at the end of the text provides students a measurement tool to judge skills they have attained.

For extra support and easy reference, an **answer key** and **glossary** are provided for students as they learn and master diagramming skills.

Author's Note

When I was growing up, I looked forward to English classes because the teachers wrote sentences on the board, while announcing, "Now take out your pencils and rulers, boys and girls, and diagram these sentences." Diagramming was fun because it meant analyzing, diagnosing, deciding, designing, and drawing . . . what modern theorists refer to as "Critical Thinking." Each of my elementary school English teachers made diagramming an exciting exercise. That excitement carried over into my later years and strengthened my enthusiasm for grammar and English.

Today some instructors are rethinking the value of diagramming. But many are returning to it simply because it is a proven method for teaching the parts of speech, helping students determine where those parts go in a sentence, and ultimately enabling them to write and speak well. Our youngsters need to communicate better. They have been processed through elementary and high schools too often exhibiting communication skills of writing and speaking that do not present them as the masters of their future, or the pacesetters required for tomorrow's leaders.

Diagramming does work to shape students' command of language, grammar, and speech. And it is to these ends that I have written this book.

Gianni DeVincentis-Hayes, Ph. D
Author

Legend

When diagramming sentences, use the key below, unless otherwise specified:

S =	Subject	**NA =**	Nouns of Address
P =	Predicate	**LV =**	Linking Verb
Expl =	Expletive	**N =**	Noun
Inj =	Interjection	**V =**	Verb
Cl =	Clause	**M =**	Modifier
Ph =	Phrase	**Adj =**	Adjective
NC =	Noun Clause	**Adv =**	Adverb
PP =	Prepositional Phrase	**Prep =**	Preposition
AP =	Appositive	**OP =**	Object of Preposition
IO =	Indirect Object	**DO =**	Direct Object
Part =	Participle	**Ger =**	Gerund
C =	Conjunction	**Inf =**	Infinitive
CC =	Coordinating Conjunction	**PA =**	Predicate Adjective
CrC =	Correlative Conjunction	**PN =**	Predicate Nominative or Predicate Noun
SC =	Subordinating Conjunction	**OC =**	Object Complement
Prn =	Pronoun	**POS =**	Parts of Speech
PresProg =	Present Progressive		

Diagnostic Exam

Diagram the following sentences. The answer key is at the back of the book.

1. Push the button.
2. The irate teacher hurriedly walked off.
3. Bob and Mary are working.
4. Mary cooks and serves.
5. Brandi was cooking and baking.
6. José and Rosella work and play.
7. When will you leave?
8. They were jailed without counsel or a phone call.
9. They sang very loudly in their high school chorus.
10. Here comes the team.
11. His gray cat is a skinny Siamese.
12. Kendra attended a cook's conference.
13. Her mother gave her a birthday present.
14. Over the hills and through the woods traveled our sled.
15. Driving to the mall, Ann stopped on the way to visit her girlfriend.
16. Pacing a room anxiously for hours may be a sign of waiting word from a loved one.
17. Courtney is working on the computer.
18. Mark is studying to pass the SATs.
19. Vote for Sam for class president.
20. Our French class and the teacher are taking a trip to beautiful Paris.
21. The best food in any restaurant often can be found in family diners.
22. Sarah sat and wrote her first book.
23. The teacher read the short story, and then he explained the plot.
24. The computer you bought is a clone.
25. This is the house that Jack built.

Diagramming sentences is a lot like working a jigsaw puzzle: You have to determine shapes or structures that go together to form a complete representation or picture of an idea or concept. In diagramming, we look at a sentence to differentiate what structures go together to give a picture of a particular thought. And while each piece in a jigsaw puzzle interlocks, so do the pieces in a sentence diagram. Everything fits together to convey an idea. Diagramming, then, connects one part of a sentence to another to give a total picture of one's thoughts, while serving as the basic structure of communication.

And just as a jigsaw puzzle solver knows the parts of a puzzle and the rules that go with putting them together, such as the frame should be built first, so it is true with those who diagram sentences to better understand the part of speech. They, too, understand that a sentence is diagrammed by first building its frame into which all the other parts fit. In knowing the parts of speech and how they interconnect and work together, we become better writers and speakers. To help with this, certain "rules" of grammar have been developed.

These rules remain essentially the same year after year, but changes are incorporated to reflect additions and deletions based on a changing world of multi-culturalism. To know what is current, it's best to look over a recent grammar text or style guide.

Sentence Framework

All sentences have two major parts: The subject and the predicate, or the verb part. These form the backbone or the frame of every unit of communication. Here is an example:

Joe walks

In this example, *Joe* is the subject, and the action word or predicate (verb) is *walks.* Thus, "Joe walks" gives us a complete picture of some character—a male—named Joe who is going somewhere. To make this image even more

Jigsaw Puzzle: Englishman John Spilsbury invented the Jigsaw Puzzle in 1760 as an educational toy to teach geography by gluing maps to thin sheets of mahogany and cutting them up.

powerful, words like *hike,* or *trod* give us a more vivid picture, as in "Joe hikes."

The subject of a sentence is always a noun, and in this case, it is a proper noun because *Joe* is the name of a person. Other proper nouns are Pittsburgh, Italy, Peach Street, Mr. Hayes, Girl Scouts of America, Tuesday. A common noun isn't capitalized, as in *man, dog, bike, people, book,* and so on. Because the subject of a sentence is a noun, it names things and tells what or whom the sentence is about.

Sometimes the subject of a sentence is "understood," meaning that though it's not written, you know it's there anyway, as in the sentence, "Come in." The subject *you* is understood to form the sentence, "You come in."

The subject of a sentence can be simple or complete. Simple subjects contain only the key word such as "Joe," while complete subjects include all the words that modify (or describe) the simple subject:

Short, chubby ten-year-old Joe

The modifiers *short, chubby, ten-year-old* tell us a little more about Joe, and thus give a clearer picture. The entire phrase, *short, chubby, ten-year-old Joe* is called the complete subject. Sometimes sentence subjects are verb forms, which will be discussed in detail in chapters 4 and 5. In diagramming, the letter S stands for Subject, and the letter N represents the word Noun. Nouns, then, are one part of speech.

And just as there are complete subjects, so are there complete predicates. The predicate part of the sentence framework relates the action, as in *walks* or *hikes.* It tells what the subject is doing. And because this part of a sentence gives the action, it's made up of a verb. The verb, then, is a word or group of words expressing the action or state of being, or the quality of belonging to a noun. Look at our example now that it has a complete predicate:

Short, chubby, ten-year-old Joe walks down the street with a pocketful of coins.

Creating a complete predicate gives an even better picture of what Joe is doing, allowing us to form an image of a youngster walking down a street,

probably to a store since he has money. The complete predicate, *walks down the street with a pocketful of coins,* adds information and color. So we've gone from a basic framework of a concept:

Joe walks.

to a more detailed picture:

Short, chubby, ten-year-old Joe walks down the street with a pocketful of coins.

Notice the punctuation in both examples. The period at the end of the sentence is called terminal punctuation, while the commas follow the modifiers. In sentence diagramming, we draw a line underneath the subject and predicate of a sentence:

Joe walks

Short, chubby, ten-year-old Joe walks down...

... the street with a pocketful of coins.

and then separate the subject from the predicate with a vertical line:

Short, chubby, ten-year-old Joe | walks down...

... the street with a pocketful of coins.

This, then, is the framework of all sentences, and the basis of all diagrams:

To determine a sentence's S and P, follow this simple formula:

1. Locate the key word that names who or what the sentence is about.

2. Locate the **action,** which tells what the "who" or "what" is doing.

3. Find words (modifiers) surrounding the "who" or the "what" in the sentence.

4. Find modifiers surrounding the "action" or the "doing" part in the sentence.

Some predicates, however, can be made up of "non-action" verbs even though they are still considered the action part of the sentence. Consider this:

Joe is young.

In this example, *Joe* is still the subject, but the predicate has been changed to the nonaction word *is.* It's called "nonaction" because it doesn't form any picture in our heads of Joe doing something, but yet it's still the verb or predicate part of the unit. *Is* is a linking verb, meaning it connects the subject to its recipient, which in this case is *young.*

There are two types of non-action verbs:
1. those made up of the verb form *to be* and other words that give passivity to a sentence; and,
2. "auxiliary" verbs or helping verbs, such as *has* and *had* and so on.

It's a good idea not to rely on passive verbs because they don't create vivid and colorful imagery, which is what good writing is all about. Chapters 3 and 4 also discuss verbs in detail.

Also remember that all sentences require a subject and predicate. If one or the other is lacking, the image becomes fragmented and thus is referred to as a fragment (frag), and is called an incomplete sentence , as in:

Short, chubby, ten-year-old Joe

This phrase doesn't tell anything about Joe, what he's doing, what action he's committing, because the predicate is missing. So this is a frag, as is this:

walks down the street with a pocketful of coins

This example lacks a subject because it doesn't tell who or what is going down the street. So a sentence must have both a subject and a predicate. Don't be fooled by phrases or clauses that **look like** they have both subjects and predicates:

Since she left her house to visit her brother

The word *she* looks like a subject, while the words *left* and *to visit* look like verbs, but yet aren't, so this is an incomplete sentence, or a frag. And while professional writers sometimes use frags for emphasis, you shouldn't do this since they're grammatically incorrect. At the other extreme are run-on or fused sentences, which have too many subjects and verbs joined together:

Mary is an expert on clothes accessories she purchased two teal colored scarves and she wore them all day long and then again at the party Jeanne held the other day for everyone who she had met in her freshmen class at college where she first met her best friend Bobbie Mary likes both Bobbie and Jeanne

In this example, one idea after another is fused or run together without proper punctuation or correct use of conjunctions.

In summary, then, make sure your thoughts are complete with a subject and a predicate and are punctuated properly, and that you use active, and not passive voice. Use diagramming as a way to picture your sentence in its proper form.

Parts of Speech

There are other parts of speech (POS) besides nouns (as subjects) and verbs (as predicates). These eight major sentence components are discussed throughout this text, but here is a list:

1. **Nouns:** name persons, places, or things; may perform in different ways, such as sentence subjects, verbals, objects, and so on; may be proper or common. (See Chap.3.)

2. **Pronouns:** substitute for nouns, so they also name persons, places, or things: he, she, they, etc. (See Chap.3.)

3. **Verbs:** tell what the person, place, or thing is doing in a sentence; may be action or nonaction (passive) in nature. (See Chap.4, 5.)

4. **Adjectives:** define or modify the meaning of a noun or pronoun; they tell what kind (**brown** eyes), which one (**that** girl), or how many (**dozen** doughnuts). (See Chap.6).

5. **Adverbs:** define or modify verbs, adjectives, or other adverbs; they tell how (walked **slowly**), where (walked **there**), when (walked **then**), and to what extent (walked **far**); adverbs often end in an -*ly* suffix: hurriedly , anxiously, eagerly, absolutely. (See Chap.6.)

6. **Prepositions:** relate a noun or pronoun to some other word in a sentence; they also introduce phrases, and they may be singular or compound: of, on, under, over, to. (See Chap.7.)

7. **Conjunctions:** are "connectors" or words that join one part of a sentence to another; these include coordinating conjunctions (yet, so), correlative conjunctions (either . . . or), and subordinating conjunctions (although, because). (See Chap.7.)

8. **Interjections:** express powerful emotions such as hate, disgust, happiness, grief, surprise, and thus are followed by an exclamation mark: Ugh! Of course! Hurry! Look out! Now! and so on. (See Chap.7.)

There are other sentence parts (such as expletives and nouns of address) that aren't listed above but are covered in this book; more on this later.

Types of Sentences

Sentences are classified by **structure** and **purpose.**

Below is classification by **purpose:**

1. **Declarative:** makes or affirms a statement or fact, and is followed by a period: Edgar Allan Poe died in Baltimore.

2. **Interrogative:** asks questions; followed by a question mark: Are we there yet?

3. **Exclamatory:** expresses strong feelings or emphasizes a point; is followed by an exclamation point; these are often interjections : I said no!

4. **Imperative:** commands or tells or orders someone to do something, and is usually followed by a period: Wait for the bus.

Below are sentences classified by **structure:**

1. **Simple:** has only one main (or independent) clause: *Dogs are lovable animals.*

S | P   One independent clause

3

2. **Compound:** has two or more independent or main clauses joined by a conjunction; it has no subordinate (or dependent) clause: *I went clothes shopping but I didn't buy anything.* The coordinating conjunction **but** joins the two main clauses.

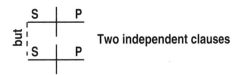

Two independent clauses

3. **Complex:** has one independent clause and at least one subordinate clause and is joined by a conjunction: *The boy became angry when his classmate hit him.* The subordinating conjunction **when** joins the two clauses.

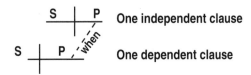

One independent clause

One dependent clause

4. **Compound-complex:** has two or more independent clauses and at least one dependent or subordinate clause, and is joined by conjunctions: *The garage that Roman had built had only one bay, so he added a second one.* The conjunctions **that** and **so** join the phrase and clause to the main sentence.

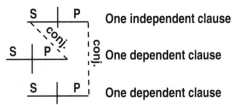

One independent clause

One dependent clause

One dependent clause

Being able to recognize sentences by their purpose or structure will help in diagramming, as well as strengthen your writing. And just as sentences can be compound in structure, so can their subjects and predicates, as in this sentence: Tamika and Tyrone are fraternal twins.

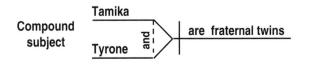

Compound subject

In this case, the compound (more than one) subject is *Tamika and Tyrone* and the complete predicate is *are fraternal twins.* However, in diagramming, the modifiers are placed on diagonal lines. The predicate, too, like its subject, may be a compound one:

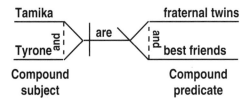

Compound subject

Compound predicate

In conclusion, a sentence contains a basic framework from which all its parts are anchored. These parts are referred to as the **Parts of Speech (POS).** Sentences may be classified by purpose or structure.

Activities

A. Underline the complete subject once, and the complete predicate twice.

Example:

David and Helen edited the school newspaper.

1. Nancy Kerrigan won the Silver Medal for skating in the 1994 Winter Olympics.
2. My Aunt Dolores makes the best pasta.
3. Sister Marilyn taught college English in 1985.
4. The thick, blinding snow paralyzed the city of Erie.
5. Isn't Ocean City, Maryland, a top, East Coast resort?
6. Margaret Garner wanted to kill her child to spare her from having to return to slavery.
7. Marta prefers studying literature over biology.
8. Holly plans on attending art school after graduating from high school.
9. All weekend long, Brynne Alysen worked on her science project.
10. Please knock before entering.

B. Classify the following sentences according to both purpose and structure, and write the proper terminal punctuation for each.

Example:

Hit the brakes! Imperative Simple

1. Tell her I said no
2. Charlotte asked for a piece of key lime pie
3. The house is on fire
4. Do you know how to use a computer
5. Look out
6. He works at an electronics company
7. There was an accident on Fifth Avenue
8. May I see the hotel manager, and will you register me in your book
9. Wow You look beautiful
10. I asked you to please come here

C. Using **S** for Subject, **N** for noun, **P** for predicate, **V** for verb, **M** for modifiers, and **PP** for prepositional phrase identify the parts in each sentence below:

Example:

S	P
N N N	V M M M

Edgar Allan Poe created many tales of the supernaturnal.

1. The osprey soared into the clouds.
2. The old man saluted the United States flag as the parade for the Vietnam soldiers marched past.
3. Heather walked slowly to the far corner of the room.
4. The pediatrician gave the child a rubella vaccination.
5. The secretary used a computer for the report.
6. The dentist filled a large cavity in my back tooth.
7. Bobby needed a passport.
8. Derrick wanted a counselor's job at the summer camp.
9. Jerry wrote a letter of complaint to the company president.
10. Pump the brakes.
11. Will you tell me the truth?
12. He's a waterman in Maryland who works the Chesapeake Bay.

D. Write **C** if the following sentences are complete, **R** if they are run-ons or fused sentences, and **FRAG** if they're incomplete; explain your reasoning (terminal punctuation and opening capitalization has been eliminated).

Example:

ring the bell
C; subject (*You*), predicate (*ring*) ; not fused or fragmented

1. according to recent research the service industry is the fastest growing field it promises the most jobs in the next decade and school career guidance counselors encourage students to take up some kind of major that will place them in the service industry when they graduate from college or vocational school that is if they want a job
2. *Challenger* exploded before everyone's eyes
3. hungry dogs pacing in waist-high cages at the humane society
4. has the teacher entered the classroom yet
5. hears well and no longer walks with a limp, or has a scar on his face
6. stories about aliens from other galaxies that originated during prehistory when dinosaurs roamed the earth
7. he won first prize a medal was given to him
8. Bob's a jogger

E. Create fifteen sentences, and
    1.) place proper terminal punctuation;
    2.) underline the simple subject;
    3.) double underline the simple predicate;
    4.) label each part of speech;
    5.) determine the type of sentence it is according to both structure and purpose.

Review

1. Effective communication is the key to properly expressing oneself, and gaining self-esteem and the respect of others.

2. All complete sentences are comprised of a S and a P; if either is missing, the resultant clause is a frag or incomplete sentence. If appropriate punctuation is missing, the sentence becomes fused or run-on.

3. Predicates are made up of action or nonaction (passive) verbs; it's better to use active verbs than passive ones.

4. There are eight major parts of speech (POS).

5. The basic framework of a sentence diagram is

6. Sentences are categorized by their structure or purpose.

POS

1. Nouns
2. Pronouns
3. Verbs
4. Adjectives
5. Adverbs
6. Prepositions
7. Conjunctions
8. Interjections

Sentence Classification

By Purpose:
1. Declarative
2. Interrogative
3. Exclamatory
4. Imperative

By Structure:
1. Simple
2. Compound
3. Complex
4. Compound-Complex

Chapter One presented sentence diagramming and how sentences could be schematically represented through the use of a horizontal line, with a vertical line separating subject from predicate. This chapter delves deeper into diagramming by discussing how the parts of a sentence are arranged graphically to fit the whole, and what the names of these parts are. This section also looks at the seven basic sentence structures, and what to do with objects.

Rules for Diagramming:

Remember, the basic sentence structure:

From here, modifiers can be placed:

They sailed in rough seas without food in the galley.

Using the horizontal line, divided by a vertical line, this sentence would look like:

They | sailed in rough seas without food in the galley.

The subject is *they,* which is both simple and complete, but the simple predicate is *sailed,* and its complete form includes everything after it.

```
      S      P
   They | sailed
```

In rough seas and *without food* and *in the galley* are prepositional phrases, which are symbolized as PP (see Chapter Seven for detailed discussion on prepositions). Their modifiers are designated as M, and their objects as OP for object of the preposition:

```
   in rough seas              in the gallery
   prep  M  OP                prep M   OP
             without food
             prep     OP
```

Prepositional phrases are diagrammed this way:

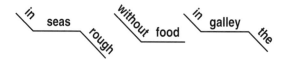

and attached to the base diagram like this:

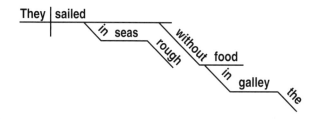

Here's another example: Bob bought a red bike with three speeds.

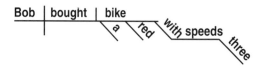

The words *a* and *red* are modifiers (which will be discussed in later chapters), and the word *bike* is the direct object (DO) because it tells what Bob bought. DOs follow the predicate and are placed on the same line. The vertical line stops right at the horizontal line.

The above models account for subjects, predicates, and their modifiers. In diagramming, each word in a sentence must be accounted for, meaning each must be placed properly and in proper order to show how one word relates to another. There are some functions that are arbitrary in diagramming, such as where to place conjunctions or indirect objects, but certain absolutes do exist and must be followed. The rules for diagramming are:

1. Read the sentence to be diagrammed. Analyze its parts of speech, and how they relate to one another:

```
            Color the sky

   S(N)   P(V)   M   DO(N)
   (You)  color  the  sky.
```

Pyramid Coin Game: Lay 10 coins out on a table in the shape of a pyramid. By moving just 3 of the coins, turn the pyramid upside down.

2. Separate the complete subject from its complete predicate:

You | color the sky.

3. Draw a horizontal line:

_____

4. Divide the line into three parts:

5. Place the subject on the first third of the line, the predicate on the second third, and the object on the third third:

6. Attach the modifiers, by diagonal lines, to the components they properly modify:

7. Check to ascertain that all the words in the sentence are diagrammed.

8. Read the completed diagram to discern that it makes sense and that each word accurately relates to the next one.

As we go along in this text, you'll see how important it is to correctly diagram sentences, because if one word is misplaced, the entire thought becomes misconstrued.

Sentence Patterns

To help diagram sentences, it's important to understand the S to P relationship, and discern what kind of sentence it is. To do this, grammarians have categorized sentences into essentially seven different types based on their patterns. These seven patterns consist of:

1. S(N) + P(V)

   S(N)   P(V)
   Margot sings.

2. S(N) + P(V) + DO(N)

   S(N)   P(V)   DO(N)
   Margot sings country songs.

3. S(N) + P(LV) + PN

   S(N)   P(LV) PN
   Margot is a singer.

4. S(N) + P(LV) + PA

   S(N)   P(PresProg) PA
   Margot is singing high.

5. S(N) + P(V) + IO(N) + DO(N)

   S(N)   P(V) IO(N) DO(N)
   Margot gave John tickets.

6. S(N) + P(V) + DO(N)+ OC(N)

   S(N)   P(V) DO(N) OC(N)
   Producer called Margot "star."

7. S(N) + P(V) + DO(N)+ OC(Adj)

   S(N)   P(V)   DO(N) OC(Adj)
   Margot dyed her shoes red.

The Simple Noun-Verb Pattern

1. S(N) + P(V)

In this first pattern, the subject, a noun, combines with the predicate, a verb, to execute a complete sentence.

        Mike laughed.
     S(N)   P(V)
    Mike | laughed

Mike is the noun or subject, and *laughed* is the verb or predicate. This example is a simple sentence with no compound subjects or compound predicates, and no modifiers, phrases or clauses. And yet, even with just two words, it's still a complete sentence.

The Noun-Verb with Direct Object Pattern

2. S(N) + P(V) + DO(N)+

A **direct object** (DO) is added in this pattern; DOs are nouns or pronouns that function as verb complements. To have a direct object, the verb or predicate must be transitive (see chapters 4 and 5). This pattern looks like:

       John painted his car.
    S(N)   P(V)   DO(N)
   John | painted | car

John is the subject or noun, *painted* is the verb or predicate, and *car* is the noun (DO) receiving the action, or telling what John painted. The pronoun *his* is a modifier, which will be discussed in the next chapter. For ease of understanding, diagramming *his* will be reserved until later. Notice the vertical line not only between the subject and predicate, but also between the predicate and the direct object; this line, however, doesn't break through the horizontal base.

The Noun-Linking Verb with Noun as Subject Complement Pattern

3. S(N)+ P(LV)+ PN

There are two major changes in this pattern: One is that the predicate is now a **linking verb** (LV), and the other is that since it is an LV, the subject needs a noun in the form of a subject complement called a Predicate Noun or Predicate Nominative (PN).

Hank was the winner.

The LV *was* links the subject, *Hank,* to the complement, *winner.* It's diagrammed this way:

```
S(N)    P(LV)    PN
Hank  |  was  \ winner
      |
```

The vertical line between the subject and the predicate is the same but the divider between the predicate and subject complement is diagonal (\) to show that it refers to the subject, *Hank*.

The Noun-Linking Verb with Adjective as Subject Complement Pattern

4. S(N) + P(LV) + PA

Like predicate nouns, which are complements of a linking verb, adjectives, too, can complement a linking verb, and, hence, they're called Predicate Adjectives (PA), and are diagrammed the same as PNs:

The cake smells delicious.
```
S(N)    P(LV)        PA
cake  | smells  \ delicious
      |
```

Cake is the subject, *smells* is the verb (a linking verb), and *delicious* is the adjective--the Predicate Adjective because its verb is linking. Notice the dividing diagonal line between the predicate and complement, as it is in the predicate noun or nominative form. The modifier *the* is an article

and an adjective (a modifier) and thus would go on a diagonal line under the word *cake* which it describes (see Chapter Six).

The Noun-Verb and Direct Object with Indirect Object Pattern

5. S(N) + P(V)+ IO(N) + DO(N)

This model is similar to the second pattern except that an Indirect Object (IO) is added, which comes **before** the direct object. Indirect objects, which are nouns or pronouns, answer the questions "for whom" or "to whom", such as:

They gave the athlete a good deal.

The indirect object is *athlete* because it tells "to whom" or "for whom" the deal was given. Indirect objects occur only with DOs (Direct Objects). They are diagrammed one of two ways:

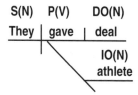

Notice how the diagonal line extends slightly past the horizontal line that the word *athlete* sits on. The second way IOs are diagrammed is:

```
S(N)     P(V)    IO(N)   DO(N)
They  |  gave  | athlete | deal
      |
```

In this model, the IO is placed on the same line as the DO, and always precedes it. Both objects have short vertical lines before them that do not break through the horizontal line. Either diagram for IOs is correct but many grammarians prefer the first model because separating the IO from the horizontal line makes it less likely to be confused with other objects. It doesn't matter which form you use but do remember that all IOs must have DOs.

The Noun-Verb and Direct Object with Noun as Object Complement Pattern

6. S(N) + P(V) + DO(N) + OC(N)

This sentence pattern has an object **following** the DO; the object may be a noun or pronoun:

Americans elected George Bush President.

The word *President* is a noun acting as the **object complement (OC),** while the name *George Bush*

behaves as the DO. Diagramming this type of sentence is easy since all the key words remain on the horizontal line:

S(N)	P(V)	DO(N)	OC(N)
American	elected	George Bush	President

To diagram this pattern, separate the predicate from the DO as you normally would, and then add a short diagonal line between the DO and the object complement. Be careful that you don't confuse the IO with the DO or the object complement (OC).

The Noun-Verb and Direct Object with Adjective as Object Complement Pattern

7. S(N) + P(V) + DO(N) + OC(Adj)

This pattern is identical to the one above except that the object complement here is an adjective instead of a noun:

Paint the kitchen green.

In this example, the subject is *you* which is understood, though not written; the verb or predicate is *paint;* the DO is *kitchen,* and the OC is *green,* which is an adjective. It's diagrammed the same way as nouns that are OCs, as depicted in the above example.

S(N)	P(V)	DO(N)	OC(Adj)
(you)	paint	kitchen	green

Again, notice the short, vertical line between the P and the DO, and the diagonal line between the DO and the OC, which signifies its reference to *paint* and *kitchen.* Just as the same type of short, vertical line is used for compound direct objects, so is the same kind of diagonal line used for compound OCs.

| Activities |

A. In the sentences below, label each part as done in this chapter, but use the letter M for modifiers:

Example :

P   IO   M   M DO   S
Give Melodie the car keys. (You)

1. Play ball.
2. My brother built a cabaña.
3. She bought the typewriter at a garage sale.
4. She offered me her C.D.
5. Hand Terry the beans.
6. Don't ask me any questions.
7. Sarah and Derrick were on the same team.
8. The television picture is blurry.
9. I visited my mother in Pittsburgh.
10. Today's not a good day.

B. Identify the main sentence pattern in each:

Example :

S   P   M   DO
I love cheese nachos.

1. The student won.
2. Choose *A* or *B*.
3. The last hurdle was the hardest.
4. The dog stole the pizza.
5. I asked you a question.
6. She nominated him president of the club.
7. Mark thought the entrance exam difficult.
8. Barbie left the door open.
9. Zeke sounded mad about the softball game.
10. I find playing billiards fun and easy.
11. Who's the vice president of this organization?
12. Call him trouble.

C. Keeping in mind the seven major sentence patterns, diagram the main framework or base of each of the following sentences, and label the parts discussed in this chapter.

Example:

S   P   DO OC(Adj.)
The kindergartener colored the cat black.

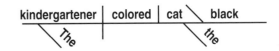

Example:

S　　P　IO　　DO　　　　　DO　　　PP
Artie gave Luke a Corvette and a certificate for free car maintenance.

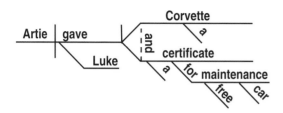

1. The animal rescue worker climbed the tree after the dog.
2. Draw a big picture of a pony.
3. The skater is exhausted.
4. Craig, George, and Kevin batted the ball around.
5. Allyce writes books, gives speeches, and sells Avon.
6. You spent too much time on this book.
7. The woman with two grown children plays piano.
8. Doctors always make me nervous.
9. Troy drives a fancy, red Mustang.
10. Kim looked pretty in her new dress.
11. Wendy and Joy won't tell him the answer.
12. I offered Alexis the sales job.

D. Read the following diagrams and translate them into their proper sentences with the correct punctuation, and identify the pattern in each:

Example:

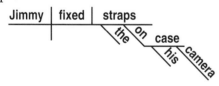

S(N) + P(V) +　DO(N)
Jimmy fixed the straps on his camera case.

1.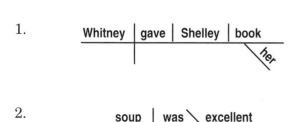

2.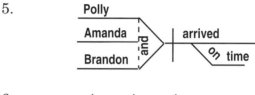

3.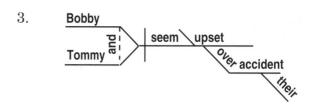

4.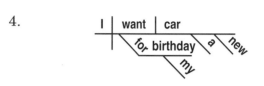

5.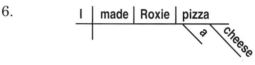

6.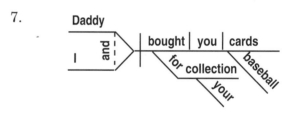

7.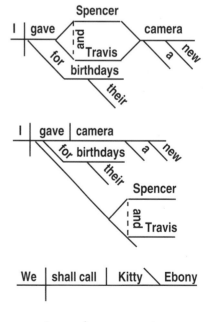

8.

9.

10.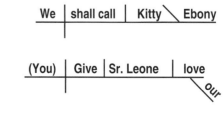

11

1. There are seven basic sentence patterns.

2. It's important to know the eight parts of speech in order to diagram sentences, and write and to speak well.

3. Complete sentences require both a subject and a predicate; if one or the other is lacking, it is called a FRAG or INC for incomplete.

The Seven Major Sentence Patterns

1. S(N) + P(V)
2. S(N) + P(V)+ DO(N)
3. S(N) + P(LV) + PN
4. S(N) + P(LV) + PA
5. S(N) + P(V) + IO(N) + DO(N)
6. S(N) + P(V) + DO(N)+ OC(N)
7. S(N) + P(V) + DO(N)+ OC(Adj)

Rules for Diagramming

1. Locate the sentence's major parts: S, P, and Complements.

2. Draw a horizontal line and place the S to the far left, and the P to the right; draw a vertical line between both that breaks through the horizontal line.

3. If there is a DO, place it after the P; insert a vertical line between it and the P.

4. If there is an IO, place it after the P and before the DO; insert a short vertical line between the P and the IO, and another **before** the DO. The IO may also be written below the horizontal line.

5. If there is an OC, place it **after** the DO, and insert a diagonal line between the DO and the object.

6. Place modifiers under the words they describe, usually on diagonal lines.

7. Learn the parts of speech, and use the legend for labeling them.

Review Test 1

I. Write C if these sentences are complete, F for fragment, and R for run-on or fused. Briefly explain your answers.

Example :

The sky became cloudy. C; has S and P

1. Dress for success.
2. Our cat, whose name is Finnegan's Rainbow, is black and white all over.
3. Add a semicolon the use of them or periods give greater clarity to the intended meaning and they're easier to read.
4. Hens that lay eggs and are used in many different foods, although they are high in cholesterol especially when fried in butter.
5. I need a new pair of eyeglasses the doctor said my vision's getting bad.
6. For the first time in five years, our basketball team—called the Bobcats—which is comprised of high school students from here in Elridge County.
7. Look!
8. The emperor's new clothes.
9. The year 2000 is destined to be pivotal in history.
10. You'll call if you need me?

II. Diagram the framework of the following sentences, and identify the sentence patterns.

Example :

Get the facts.

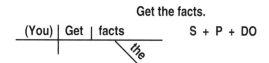

S + P + DO

1. The little girl behind me cried at the loss of her dog.
2. The irate patron suddenly walked off.
3. Carl and Brian play baseball and jog.
4. Where have you been?
5. Barbara sang quite well.
6. The parasailor soared quickly, and silently flew away.
7. Our cock-a-poo is black.
8. Don't eat so fast.
9. Kelsey's softball team practices every day.
10. Are you the band director?
11. Well! I never!
12. Fire!
13. She looks pretty in white.
14. The freshman class elected Bart leader.
15. The waves ripped through the resort area.
16. Give the hummingbird nectar.

17. John Wayne's real name was Marion Morrison.
18. Count your blessings.
19. Master Maid, Country Caterers, and Mr. Clean cook and clean.
20. Sam and Greg are playing hockey.

III. Fill in the chart according to the subject, predicate, and complements.

Sentence	S	P	O
Example: **Max gave John his best glove.**	Max	gave	John = IO glove = DO
1. NPR broadcasts some unusual and insightful programs.			
2. Regia experiences panic attacks at great heights.			
3. Leslie wants to be an actress.			
4. Clichés erode good writing.			
5. The Senate declared the law unconstitutional in 1899.			
6. How do you find the defendant—guilty or not guilty?			
7. Kara's a wonderful neighbor and babysitter.			
8. Under the circumstances, Jessica considers herself lucky.			
9. All nine girls think their baseball team the best.			
10. The drama teacher determined the students' suggestions too costly.			
11. I never thought myself shy.			
12. Jake's party was a huge success; he gave it on the Fourth of July.			
13. Marty and Harry are the only two male nurses on the floor.			
14. See that flower over there?			
15. The UPS delivery person handed Margaret two packages.			
16. Bring a stack of pancakes here.			

IV. Identify each function using S, P, IO, DO, PN, PA, LV, PP, and M.

Example :

M   S   P   PP   M
No letters were in the mail today.

1. Please make me address labels on your computer.
2. Didn't you staple those papers in that pile?
3. Ken's buying a house on the water.
4. Everyone's worrying about the pollution in Puget Sound.
5. Spring forward, and fall back.

14

6. Some T.V. networks offer only mindless programs.

7. New York City is one of the best cities for national and international businesses.

8. My family went on a trip through the New England area.

9. Saint John's junior class produced and presented *My Fair Lady*.

10. Sam and Greg are playing hockey.

11. Help me!

12. Perry Como comes from Canonsburg.

13. I bought the red roses but the vase was given to me.

14. Maxine and Rolanda escaped the fire without getting burned.

15. Diagramming sentences requires critical thinking.

V. Identify according to function and structure, and punctuate correctly.

Sentence	Function	Structure	Punctuation
Example:			
I wanted to buy a new bike, but I settled for a used one.	declarative	compound	period
1. Could you please see me			
2. I said no			
3. Put mayonnaise on it, too			
4. watch			
5. Didn't he write that book, too			
6. Call the fire department			
7. Mary can't imagine anyone wanting to study that, but then she never did like science			
8. David's a computer specialist who even works on weekends			
9. Chef Ana Lina directs the kitchen staff, but she also likes to cook			
10. The loser was Zebulon			
11. Call me Dr. Jones			
12. The parents named their baby Chad			
13. Did you call me a fool			
14. We dyed the eggs green and gold			
15. They called their dog Rufus			
16. Louie's too young to date			
17. I'm exhausted			
18. She laughs hard			
19. Tom and Chelsea left quickly, but they'll be back soon			
20. And that ends this test			

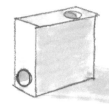

So far we've concentrated on sentence types and the basics of diagramming. This chapter looks at nouns and pronouns, and briefly reviews contractions. As stated in Chapter One, nouns name things, people, places, and qualities or ideas. They're found in the singular form (goose), the plural (geese), the collective (gaggle), the possessive (goose's), as well as in the concrete and abstract forms. Pronouns, on the other hand, substitute for nouns.

Nouns

Anything that can be named (objects, feelings, people, places, ideas, qualities, states) is a **noun.** They're identified in a sentence based on their location in the arrangement of words:

S(N)	P(V)
John	dances

Since the name of someone or something generally comes before the verb, we realize then that *John* is a noun. This is also true with objects which come after verbs:

S(N)	V(P)	IO(N)	DO(N)
Bob	gave	Peggy	a letter

So a sentence's structure also gives clues as to its parts of speech. Thus, we can recognize nouns based on these criteria:

1. **Names persons:** man, Mrs. Jones, John, Sister Katherine
2. **Names places:** Brazil, Los Alamos, the Yukon
3. **Names things:** boxes, cars, books, letters
4. They often **follow** determiners such as *the, an, a, my, this:* the *child,* an *apple.*
5. They **follow** prepositions as objects (objects of prepositions [OPs]): before *he,* on the *shelf,* above the *sink,* of *California.*

6. They may have various endings: *-ness* (soundness), *-ity* (mendacity), *-tion* (approbation), *-ship* (apprenticeship), *-phy* (demography).
7. They occur **before** or **after** verbs: *car* accelerates.
8. They may take an apostrophe: the *girl's* dress.
9. They may serve as appositives: Mary, *my cousin,* or as modifiers, *school* bus.

Nouns may be common or proper. If they don't specify a particular person, place, or thing, they're called **common**, and aren't capitalized:

son	sheriff	town	book
college	professor	stadium	ambassador
program	mother	school	judge

But if a particular person, place, or thing is named, it becomes **proper** and is capitalized:

John	Sheriff Tom	Amityville	*Love Story*
UCLA	Professor Lin	Shea Stadium	S. Temple
Al-Anon	Mother Teresa	Kennedy High	O'Connor

Proper nouns are always capitalized, and they name such things as continents (Asia), days of the week (Monday), holidays (Fourth of July), months (June), countries (Peru), cities (Dayton), titles (Princess Diana), festivals (Oktoberfest), people (Paula), regions (Northwest), states (Maine), rivers (Missouri), nationalities (Italian), religions (Buddhism), organizations (Girl Scouts), planets (Jupiter), buildings (U.S. Mint), and so on.

Nouns can be **singular** or **plural.** Singular nouns name one person, place, or thing, while plural nouns name more than one, and are formed by adding an *-s* or *-es* or *-ies.*

Singular Nouns	Plural Nouns
house	houses
box	boxes
fox	foxes
farmer	farmers
penny	pennies
sky	skies
sigh	sighs
fairy	fairies

Takitapart Puzzle: Patented in the U.S., it consists of 4 square blocks, 2 interlocking bars and 4 pins or dowels. The object is to take the puzzle apart to retrieve the partially visible penny.

Some nouns change in form when made plural:

Plural Nouns that Change in Form

appendix	appendices	or	appendixes
formula	formulae	or	formulas
curriculum	curricula	or	curriculums
hoof	hoofs	or	hooves

goose	geese	thesis	theses
fungus	fungi	focus	foci
ox	oxen	datum	data
criterion	criteria	tooth	teeth
child	children	algae	alga

But some nouns represent singular or plural based on how they're used in a sentence:

deer	pair	fruit	fish

Contrarily, there are nouns that always remain in the plural:

mathematics	trousers	cattle	headquarters
pants	scissors	ethics	politics

Nouns may be concrete or abstract. A concrete noun refers to something tangible, while abstract nouns express emotions, the five senses, or ideas:

Concrete Nouns		Abstract Nouns	
bread	Mt. Etna	fear	secret
Red Sea	White House	Saturday	belief
Mars	comet	wish	humor
fish	car	music	blue
camera	computer	liberty	friendship
Irishman	T.V.	love	religion

There are nouns, called collective, that represent a group of things or people:

Collective Nouns

council	group	flock	team
audience	bevy	nation	public
parish	slate	school	citizenry
union	bunch	herd	congregation
faculty	state	board	organization
family	ballot	jury	populace
panel	club	class	orchestra
gaggle	pack	band	committee
clergy	batch	crowd	community

To show ownership or possession, add apostrophe and 's' to the noun:

boy's glove	children's room	bike's lock

If a word doesn't end in an *s* or if it has a *z* sound, add only the apostrophe:

babies' toys	boys' school	trees' bark

Although objects can't own anything, many phrases have become common today, such as:

razor's edge	day's work	story's plot

Always refer to a dictionary to determine what's correct. There are four main ways nouns may be used:

As subjects: to tell who or what is being talked about:

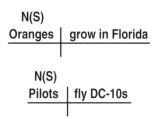

As objects: may be used as (a.) direct object, (b.) indirect object, (c.) object of preposition, (d.) object complement; objects complete the action of the verb, and tell what or whom about it:

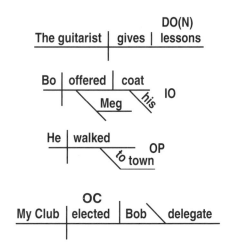

As predicate noun or nominative: to link S to P, and follow a linking verb:

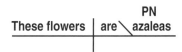

As modifiers: nouns describe, and they are placed on diagonal lines:

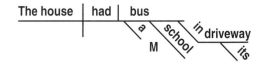

In summary, then, nouns have a variety of qualities and functions. Pronouns are a close kin.

Pronouns

Words such as *his, my, ours,* are **pronouns.** They serve to substitute or stand in for nouns. It's important, though, to make the reference to the noun clear. Consider this:

Marta put her books in her locker.

This example is clear because there's only one *her,* but look what happens when we complicate matters by writing:

Marta put her books in her locker, and at dismissal, she and her friend went to her locker and slipped them into her book bag to take home with her.

With too many pronouns substituting for nouns, the sentence becomes unclear. So when working with pronouns, take care that the reference to the specific noun is distinct.

Personal Pronouns refer to a person, and may be used in three ways. They make up the largest group of pronouns.

1. Reference to the person speaking:
   I ate my lunch.

2. Reference to people, places, or things:
   They brought their books with them.

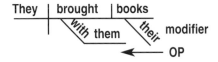

3. Reference to someone spoken to:
   Have you given your speech?

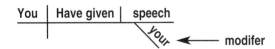

Personal pronouns may be singular or plural:

Singular	Plural	Singular	Plural
I	we	your, yours	your, yours
me	us	my, mine	our, ours
you	you	he, him, his	they
she, her, hers	they, them	it	
	their, theirs		

Although nouns don't change when used in different ways, pronouns do, depending on their use. They can function in three ways:

1. As the subject:

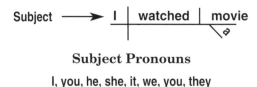

Subject Pronouns

I, you, he, she, it, we, you, they

2. As an object:

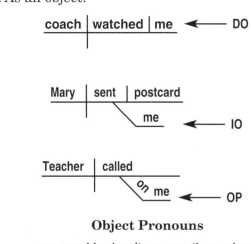

Object Pronouns

me, you, him, her, it, us, you, them, whom

3. As a modifier (showing possession):

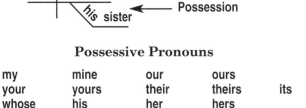

Possessive Pronouns

my	mine	our	ours	
your	yours	their	theirs	its
whose	his	her	hers	

The possessive form of a pronoun shows ownership or "belonging," and may be used as the subject of a trans verb or as the predicate nominative, which comes from linking verbs; predicate pronouns are the most misused of all the pronouns:

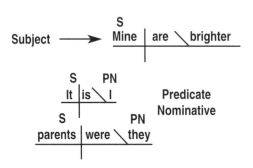

19

Besides those pronouns already discussed, there are other types:

1. Relative pronouns: substitute for a repeated noun:

   Without the relative pronoun: Terry Bradshaw—Terry Bradshaw was one of the best quarterbacks—is now a sports commentator.

   With relative pronoun: Terry Bradshaw—who was one of the best quarterbacks—is now a sports commentator.

Relative Pronouns

People	Things
who, whom, whose	which, that

Relative pronouns are also called interrogative pronouns because most of them ask a question. And some pronouns crossover into other types of speech.

2. Demonstrative pronouns: refer to the distance from, or nearness to the speaker, and they point out people or objects:

   nearness: This is the book. These gifts are for you.
   distance: Those are my coupons. That is my purse.

Demonstrative Pronouns

This, these, that, those

3. Indefinite pronouns: don't refer to any particular or "definite" person or thing. Their antecedents (the persons or things they refer to) are vague:

   Is anything the matter?   **Everyone has plans.**
   Both bought red scarves.   **Many feel scared.**
   All of the cake is iced.   **All the plants blossomed.**

Indefinite pronouns may be singular, plural, or either.

Indefinite Pronouns

Singular		Plural	Either
anything	either	both	all
another	everybody	many	none
everyone	everyone	few	some
anybody	each	several	more
anyone	one		most
everything	somebody		any
someone	nobody		
no one	neither		

4. Reflexive pronouns: are those ending in *-self* or *-selves*. They reflect or refer to the subject of the verb, meaning the subject and object are one.

   Dustin had only himself to blame.

   Dustin had himself —— reflexive

Because these types of pronouns put emphasis on the subject, they're also called intensive pronouns and compound personal pronouns, since they're made up of two words.

Reflexive/Intensive Pronouns

yourself	yourselves	itself	myself
ourselves	himself	herself	themselves

Contractions

Contractions are formed by combining a verb and a pronoun, while omitting one or more letters; the omission is represented by an apostrophe. Contractions are acceptable in informal writing and speech. Here's an example: you + are = you're

The apostrophe shows that the letter *a* in *are* is omitted. Don't confuse contractions with the possessive form of pronouns. Here's a comparison:

Sample Contractions

it + is = it's	who + would = who'd
you + are = you're	I + would = I'd
they + are = they're	you + have = you've
who + is = who's	I + am = I'm
we + have =we've	you + will = you'll

Possessive Pronouns

its
your
their
whose

A contraction may be diagrammed by:

1. Breaking it down into its original form:

   I've been looking for you.

I	have been looking

2. Writing it on the diagonal line:

   Margeaux isn't my friend.

   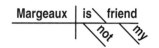

20

In conclusion, we can see the vital role pronouns play in relating the importance of nouns, and how contractions make speech flow smoothly and informally.

Activities

A. Underline all nouns once, pronouns twice, contractions three times. Correct proper nouns that aren't capitalized.

Example:

You'll give a quarter to Mr. Cummings?

1. My mother has macular degeneration, an eye disorder.
2. Kenny got a counselor's job at my brother's summer camp.
3. It's up to you.
4. Her garden needs weeding.
5. Horton's Pharmacy has your prescription filled.
6. Tracy and vince themselves designed their own wedding.
7. Have you practiced your lines for the play?
8. Will somebody answer me—whoever is there?
9. The president offered nancy and me a job with the company.
10. Mine are heavier and larger.

B. Circle the word in each sentence that will correctly complete it.

Example:

(Its, It's) not up to (she, her).

1. That was (she, her)
2. It was (he, him) who answered the door.
3. (Its, It's) entirely up to you.
4. My teacher gave the job to (me, I).
5. Each of (we, us) had our own desk.
6. The house was built by Alex and (they, them).
7. Will you give this address to (she, her)?
8. Was it (they, them) who won?
9. They rated (theirselves, themselves) an A.
10. He, (hisself, himself), painted the car.

C. Tell whether each of the italicized pronouns is in subject or object form.

Example:

Becky is older than *she*. subject

1. Michael is taller than *he*.
2. It was *they* who decorated the tree.
3. He teaches as well as *I*.
4. Linda and *I* are going to the mall.
5. Hand it to *whoever* comes next.
6. I don't know *who* stole the house keys.
7. *Whom* were they referring to?
8. Give it to *whomever* he names.
9. Many of *us* watched the movie.
10. Placing *me* before *her* made *me* feel guilty.

D. Diagram the following sentences and circle the pronouns.

Example:

He wants to dance with me.

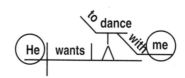

1. This is the right way.
2. Who's the lady with Peter?
3. That is an Air Force plane.
4. She and I work hard and play tirelessly.
5. The pie came from my neighbor.
6. All of us took English 101.
7. Who's reading the book?
8. Sleep soundly.
9. He or she will give us the album.
10. We come from New York City.

Review

1. Nouns name things, people, places, ideas, and qualities; pronouns substitute for nouns.

2. Nouns may be made plural by adding "s," or they may change form entirely.

3. Nouns that show ownership are possessive; nouns that represent a group of the same kind are collective; nouns that refer to tangible things, places, people are concrete; and nouns that refer to feelings or expressions are abstract.

4. Pronouns may be relative (or interrogative), demonstrative, indefinite, or reflexive (also called intensive and compound personal pronouns).

5. Contractions are acceptable in informal writing.

Overview of Three Major Pronoun (Forms) Cases

Subject	Object	Possessive
I	me	my, mine
they	them	their, theirs
you	you	your, yours
we	us	our, ours
he	him	his
she	her	her, hers
it	it	its
who	whom	whose

Ways Nouns and Nominals Function in Sentences

S   DO   OP   IO   OC   PN   AP

Ways Personal Pronouns Function in Sentences

1. reference to speaker
2. reference to people, places, things
3. reference to someone spoken to

Types of Pronouns

relative   demonstrative   indefinite   reflexive

CHAPTER 4  Verbs I

Verbs are the "do-ers" or the action part of a sentence. This chapter begins an overview of verbs, which concludes with Chapter Five. The focus here will be on diagramming transitive verbs, although other characteristics of verbs will be discussed. Please note that this chapter is not meant to be an exhaustive analysis of verbs.

Verb Types and Characteristics

Verbs are the predicates in a sentence; they function in expressing action, or helping to complete a thought or statement. There are two major verb forms: transitive and intransitive. Additionally, verbs have characteristics specific to them; these include:

1. Voice: Verbs can have active or passive voice. While transitive verbs *often* make the voice active, intransitive verbs *may* make the voice passive, but not necessarily for both in all instances.

Compare the two model sentences to follow, one is active and one is passive.

Active: The boy batted the ball.

The subject–"boy"–is doing the action. The voice is transitive. Active voice should show action, meaning that the subject is the preformer, and not the receiver of the action. The "boy" is doing the action–"batting."

Passive: The ball was batted by the boy.

Here, the linking verb "was" is the past tense of the verb form "to be," making the sentence passive because the subject, "ball," is acted upon rather than preforming the action. At times, the preposition, "by," gives a clue that the sentence may be passive.

Passive verbs (intransitive sentences) may have a *compliment*. Active verbs (intransitive sentences) will have *direct objects*.

2. Mood: This is another property of a verb that conveys a writer's attitude toward what he or she is writing. There are four major verb moods: indicative, imperative, subjunctive, and interrogative.

Indicative mood: makes a statement of fact, or an assertion.

Example:

Trevor showers in the morning.

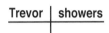

Imperative mood: makes a command, gives orders. It's authoritative in nature.

Example:

Go to the store and get me milk.

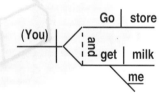

Subjunctive mood: issues statements of hope, or makes a wish, a supposition, or possibility; verbs like *might* or *should* show hope or possibility and are good indicators of this mood.

Example:

If he were here, we could leave early.

Example:

If she were a gifted writer, she would write a best-seller.

Interrogative mood: asks a question.
Example:
Will he walk home?

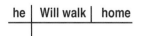

3. Mode: This third verb characteristic expresses emotions, feelings, or ideas. Look at these examples to better understand the mode of verbs.

Dad's Puzzler: First appearing in 1909, Dad's Puzzler (Few solve it, but it can be done.) was one of many sliding block puzzles with the object of moving one block to the opposite corner without jumping or removing any block, or turning any piece.

a. fact:	He lied about his income.
b. intent:	The sun will rise tomorrow.
c. ability:	She could play piano by ear.
d. permission:	You may help us.
e. necessity:	I must see the doctor now.
f. conclusion:	On the basis of the evidence, he must have been the murderer.
g. courage:	He dared to be great.

4. Tense: Verbs have different forms. Depicting forms in each of its tenses is called **conjugation.** The tense of verbs tells time, or when something happened or will happen. Here are the verb tenses:

Present:	I walk
Past:	I walked
Past Participle:	I walked
Present Progressive:	I am walking
Present Perfect:	I have walked
Past Progressive:	I was walking
Past Perfect:	I had walked
Future:	I will walk
Future Progressive:	I will have been walking
Future Perfect:	I will have walked

Irregular verbs are conjugated a bit differently. They take a "sound" change as seen here:

present	past	past participle ("have")
ring	rang	rung
feel	felt	felt
swim	swam	swum
lend	lent	lent
break	broke	broken
begin	began	begun
lie	lay	lain
set	set	set

5. Person/Number: This last verb property deals with how many people are speaking or being referred to. In writing, we must choose from which perspective or point-of-view (POV) to tell a story or relate a message. A verb is dependent upon this perspective or person. There are three main persons (or viewpoints) which is referred to as **number.**

1. singular, first-person	=	I
2. singular, second-person	=	you
3. singular, third-person	=	he, she, it
1. plural, first-person	=	we
2. plural, second-person	=	you
3. plural, third-person	=	they

Verbs must agree with this number; thus, this would be incorrect: We walks. Before moving on to diagramming transitive verbs, let's capsulize what has been presented thus far:

Characterizing the Verb *Talk*

Infinitive:	to talk
Present tense:	I talk
Past tense:	I talked
Past participle:	I talked
Future tense:	I will talk
Present progressive:	I am talking
Present perfect:	I have talked
Past progressive:	I was talking
Past perfect:	I had talked
Future progressive:	I will have been talking
Future Perfect:	I will have talked

Voice	Mood	Mode	Person/#
active:	Indicative:	Intent:	Singular:
Babs talked	I talked	Babs will talk	I talk
passive:	Imperative:	Capability:	you talk
The talking was	Talk to me!	He could talk	he, she,
done by Babs.	Subjunctive:	Necessity:	it talks
	If I had talked	I must talk	Plural:
	Interrogative:	Permission:	we talk
	Will you talk?	You may talk	you talk
		Conclusion:	they talk
		You must have	
		been the talker	
		Courage:	
		He dare talk	
		Fact:	
		John did talk	

Transitive Verbs

Transitive and intransitive verbs are also discussed in Chapter 5. Transitive verbs "transfer" the action to their complements. There are three kinds of complements or objects:

1. Direct Objects: All transitive verbs have direct objects (DOs), but only certain verbs have indirect objects (IOs) or object complements. DOs are persons or things that "receive" the verb's action. They answer the questions what or whom, such as:

Draw a line.

S(N)	P(V)	DO(N)
(You)	Draw	line

In this example, the DO is *line* because it tells what to draw. The word *line* receives the action of the verb *draw*. DOs don't answer how, when, or where, such as: Mary came quickly, in which the word *quickly* tells how, and is an adverb. In the above diagram, notice where the DO is placed, which is immediately **after** the predicate. Here's another example:

Don't newscasters announce events?

To tell what the DO is, ask **what** do newscasters announce? The answer is *events.*

```
      S(N)            P(V)          DO(N)
  Newscasters  |  Do announce  |  events
                        |
```

The word *current* modifies *events* and thus goes on a diagonal line. *Not* is an adverb modifying the verb and is also placed on a diagonal line underneath the predicate. Notice that DOs are nouns. By knowing the parts of speech, you'll understand where they go in a diagram, and how to use them in a sentence when speaking or writing.

2. Indirect Objects are another type of complement coupled with transitive verbs. All IOs require DOs. IOs answer for whom, to whom, and for what, to what.

My parents bought me a new skateboard.

In this example, the IO, *me,* answers for whom. When diagramming this sentence, you may place the IO on a horizontal line below the verb (attached by a diagonal line with a slight extension):

```
  parents  |  bought  |  skateboard
                  \
                   me
```

But another way to diagram the IO is to place it on the **same** line as the DO, right after the predicate, and right before the DO:

```
    S(N)      P(V)     IO(N)    DO(N)
  parents |  bought  |  me  |  skateboard
      \        |                  \
```

A short vertical line separates the predicate from the IO, and another short vertical line divides the IO from its DO. Either method is correct, but placing the IO on a diagonal line below the verb prevents any mix up with the DO. Nouns and pronouns can be IOs, as below:

Harvey told Alex *(or him)* the bad news.

```
  Harvey  |  told  |  Alex  |  news
                |              \  \
```

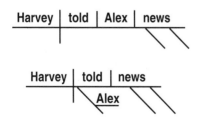

```
  Harvey  |  told  |  news
                      \  \
              \  Alex
```

A third and final type of transitive verb complement is the:

3. Object Complement: This type of object completes the meaning of a thought. It always refers to the DO. Object complements (OC) come **after** the DO in a sentence, and they may be adjectives or nouns. Here are examples of adjectives as OCs:

Paint the car green.

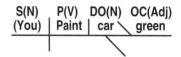
```
    S(N)    P(V)   DO(N)   OC(Adj)
  (You)  |  Paint  |  car  \  green
                              \
```

Marta thought the citizenship exam tricky.

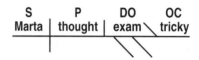
```
     S         P        DO      OC
  Marta  |  thought  |  exam  \  tricky
                |          \
```

Does Andre think his office-mate pretty?

```
     S          P            DO         OC
  Andre  |  Does think  |  office-mate  \  pretty
                |               \
```

Nouns as object complements are diagrammed the same way as adjective OCs:

They called their cat Charlie.

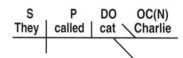
```
     S        P        DO      OC(N)
  They  |  called  |  cat  \  Charlie
                            \
```

Sid and Char picked and named Cal and Rich leaders and directors.

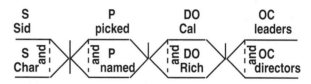
```
    S           P            DO          OC
  Sid        picked         Cal        leaders
   \   and    \   and   P    \   and  DO  \  and OC
  Char         named         Rich        directors
```

In summary, then, transitive verbs are action verbs that may take direct objects. They also may have IOs but they **must** have DOs. As action verbs, the action of the transitive predicate may be physical (kick, jump, cook, snap), abstract (possess, inspire, intend), or intellectual (calculate, choose, synthesize, analyze).

A verb that isn't transitive, must then be intransitive, or not an action verb. Intransitive verbs do **not** take objects. These will be discussed in detail in the next chapter. Linking verbs can make a sentence active or passive but more commonly such sentences are likely to result in passive voice.

Activities

A. Fill in the chart below based on the predicate's properties (some may be arbitrary).

Sentence	Voice	Mood	Mode	Tense	Person
Example:					
Sheila's mother worries	active	ind	fact	present	3rd-s
1. George leaped over the fence					
2. Answer me					
3. Was Zeke talking to him					
4. I'll answer any question					
5. If I were you, I wouldn't have done that					
6. They darted through back streets					
7. You must elect him president					
8. Julie and Joel swam daily					
9. Heather will have earned highest grades					
10. It just can't be done					
11. She will have been playing almost two hours					
12. I'm considering changing jobs					

B. Underline the transitive verbs in the sentences below; identify complements by writing DO for direct object, IO for indirect object, OC(Adj) for object complements that are adjectives, or OC(N) for object complements that are nouns.

Example.

DO OC(Adj)
The present <u>made</u> her happy.

1. Travis and Brianna baptized their first child Carrie Marie.
2. Grandma made me Toll House cookies.
3. Pass me the ketchup please.
4. My brother figures out math problems on his computer.
5. The teen painted his Prelude a neon red.
6. We nominated Bubba "Most Valuable Player."
7. Chandler, Tom, and Cheynie painted their club house gingerbread brown.
8. Do you think me pretty?
9. We never thought her a good teacher.
10. Dr. Stockard considered her college class rude and loud.
11. My Uncle Harry bought the stereo cheap.
12. Rover and Fido did tricks and jumped hoops.

13. She called him lazy and spoiled.
14. Maxine thought the song melodious.
15. Consider her a failure.
16. The mail carrier gave her a letter.
17. Did you play that tune on the piano or on the organ?

C. Diagram the following sentences, and label all the parts so far discussed; use M for modifiers, PP for prepositional phrases.

Example:

Mark gave me his best drawing, and he had painted it a deep green and purple.

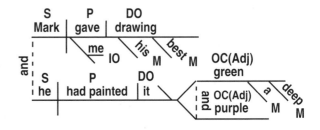

1. Julio painted the flag red, white, and blue.
2. The tale about the raven made me scared.
3. Will you shut the door?

26

4. Donnie called his van "Turbo."

5. Bessie thinks her condo beautiful.

6. The club thought the speaker excellent.

7. Brynne's referee called her safe.

8. Marlo imagined the book's murderer tall, heavy, and bearded.

9. The Three Musketeers handed me their swords.

10. Ask your teacher those questions.

11. Send me a copy.

12. Gramps built Zeb a tackle box.

13. Mrs. Black sold you a fax machine.

14. Will you give that teen a job?

15. Don't give him any answers.

16. Will you send her flowers?

17. The police officer and firefighter showed us the way out.

18. The class voted her "outstanding" and "class wit."

19. The fraternity brothers left the house a wreck.

20. The governor announced Groundhog Day a holiday in Pennsylvania.

D. Make a list of ten action verbs and ten passive verbs. (Answers will vary.)

Example:

Active Verbs	Passive Verbs
1. jumped	1. feel
2. skated	2. become
3. skidded	3. smell
4. pulsed	4. be

Review

1. Verbs may be **active** or **passive,** and are divided into two main categories: **transitive** and **intransitive.** They have properties and characteristics of their own such as **mood, voice, mode, tense,** and **number** or **person.**

2. Verbs can be regular or irregular. Irregular verbs are conjugated differently.

3. **Transitive** verbs "transfer" their action to their "complements." There are three types of complements: Direct objects (DO), indirect objects (IO), object complements (OC). Transitive verbs may denote physical action, intellectual action, or abstract action.

4. All transitive verbs have DOs. DOs are persons or things that receive action; they answer what or whom, and are nouns or pronouns. In a diagram, they follow the predicate.

5. IOs answer to whom or for whom, and to what or for what. In a diagram, they may be placed on a diagonal line under the predicate or on the horizontal line after the predicate and before the DO. IOs are usually proper nouns or pronouns. A DO must be present whenever an IO exists.

6. OCs are either nouns or adjectives. They complete the meaning of a sentence and always require a DO, which they follow.

Verb Characteristics or Properties

1. Voice: active or passive

2. Mood: indicative, imperative, subjunctive, interrogative

3. Mode: fact, intent, capability, permission, necessity, conclusion, courage

4. Tense: present, past, past participle, present progressive, present perfect, past progressive, past perfect, future, future progressive, future perfect

5. Person: Singular: 1st, 2nd, 3rd; Plural: 1st, 2nd, 3rd

Transitive Verb Complements

1. Direct Objects (DO): persons or things receiving action; DOs can be present with transitive verbs. DOs are nouns, and are diagrammed this way:

```
  S    P     DO
 Bob | drew | house
```

2. Indirect Objects (IO): tell to whom the action is directed; they may be nouns or pronouns, and are diagrammed on a diagonal line below the predicate, or on the horizontal line between the P and the DO:

```
  S    P    IO   DO             S    P     DO
 Luis | gave | me | candy      Luis | gave | candy
   |                                      \ me
                                            IO
```

3. Object Complements (OC): complete a thought's meaning, and always refer to the DO. They are nouns or adjectives, and are diagrammed like this:

```
 S      P     DO  OC(N)          S      P    DO OC(Adj)
He | called | him \ Jeb       (You) | Color | me \ sad
```

I. Underline nouns once, pronouns twice; write PRP over proper nouns (capitalization has been omitted). Correct capitalization, and diagram and label the Ss and Ps.

Example:

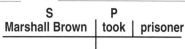

PRP   PRP
marshal brown took the prisoner to the eastern shore correctional institute for incarceration.

S   P
Marshall Brown | took | prisoner

Example:

he's been a marshall for a long time.

S   P
He | has been \ marshall

1. emily dickinson was a great poet.
2. martin found his wallet in his pants pocket.
3. the pittsburgh steelers won four super bowls.
4. the caribbean sea is filled with jewels of underwater life.
5. meg and i are lambda chi rho sorority sisters who live at the riverside sorority house.
6. we'll get you a new clock radio since your brother broke your last one.
7. ocean city, maryland, is a family resort on the coast.
8. the manta ray is a large animal living in tropical waters.
9. a hovercraft is a vehicle that travels in air, over water, and on smooth ground surfaces.
10. a system of reading for the blind is called braille.
11. the author edgar allan poe died in baltimore; his works are often bizarre and eerie.
12. broadway is the theater district of new york city
13. ho chi minh city is the capital of south vietnam; it used to be called saigon.
14. go!
15. will you watch little gregory for me tonight?

II. Change singular nouns to plural, and plural nouns to singular.

Example:

fox = foxes; bike = bikes

1. medium   = _____
2. churches = _____
3. criteria = _____
4. penny   = _____
5. hooves   = _____
6. geese   = _____
7. deer   = _____
8. crises   = _____

9. parenthesis = _____
10. foci   = _____
11. teeth   = _____
12. datum   = _____
13. curricula = _____
14. cherub   = _____
15. knives   = _____
16. fungus   = _____

III. Form the possessives of the following nouns:

Example:

babies toys = babies'

1. girls dresses = _____
2. child playroom = _____
3. dogs bone = _____
4. fox den = _____
5. knifes handle = _____

6. razors = _____
7. quarters = _____
8. man = _____
9. author = _____
10. kids = _____

IV. Label nouns, pronouns and proper nouns in each sentence. Then diagram and label each sentence (eliminate modifiers). Capitalize sentences and diagrams as necessary.

Example:

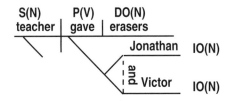

1. *little women* is a movie classic.
2. tom clancy wrote the best-selling novel, *the hunt for red october*.
3. barry didn't offer a pregnant woman his seat on the bus.
4. the guitar teacher gave mary ellen lessons on thursdays.
5. the trees in her backyard were dogwoods and cherries.
6. barbara stanwyck was a famous actress.
7. you and he were funny.
8. mine are better.
9. didn't you finish?
10. this isn't the catalogue here.
11. everyone was friendly.
12. no one has been around here.
13. all of the flowers are blossoming.
14. the writers' organization considered the presenter on book publishing excellent.
15. don't you care?

V. Translate into sentences. Label POS (use legend in this book); use M for modifiers.

Example.

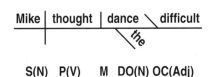

S(N) P(V) M DO(N) OC(Adj)
Mike thought the dance difficult.

1.

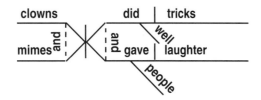

2.

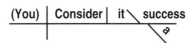

3.

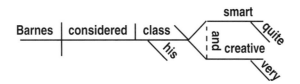

4.

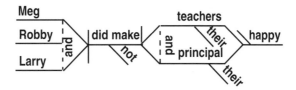

5.

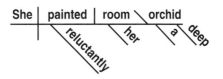

VI. Fill in this chart according to the verbs' properties or characteristics.

Sentences	Voice	Mood	Mode	Tense	Person
Example:					
The panel elected her "Miss Teen."	active	ind	fact	past	3rd-s
1. Will you help me now?					
2. She could throw the javelin far.					
3. Based on what you told me, I think it's true.					
4. She braved the fire to save the child.					
5. You must read this.					
6. You can do it; I just know it.					
7. Marty will be speaking first tomorrow.					
8. Pick up your room.					
9. If you were to dismiss us early, I could make it.					
10. Buddy is a gray cat.					

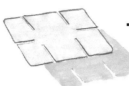

The last chapter discussed transitive or action verbs, and how these verbs took objects and complements. This chapter looks at intransitive and linking verbs. Intransitive verbs do not need objects or complements to complete their meaning. Additionally, this chapter looks at verbals, which are words that appear to be verbs but instead behave as other parts of speech. This chapter is not meant to be an extensive study of verbs.

Intransitive vs Transitive Verbs

In the examples below, compare how transitive verbs require objects to complete their meaning to intransitive verbs which don't.

transitive:

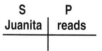

S	P	DO
Allysen	joined	club

In the above, the word *club* is required to complete what Allysen joined; and since objects answer questions of what, *club,* then, is a direct object (DO). So an object is needed to finish the thought. But this isn't the case with intransitive verbs:

intransitive:

S	P
Jack	is swimming

As this sentence stands, it makes sense. No object is needed to complete its meaning, so the predicate, *is swimming,* is complete in itself. And *is* is a linking verb. Intransitive verbs don't need DOs. Consider these examples of intransitive verbs:

Talia and George are eating by candlelight.

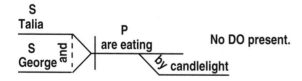

No DO present.

In this example, there is no DO, and the predicate is a linking verb; however, some action words can also be intransitive:

Juanita reads in the afternoon.

S	P
Juanita	reads

The word *reads* is an action verb, but in this case it's intransitive since it doesn't take an object. But in "Juanita reads a book," the verb has the object *book,* and thus is transitive. Linking verbs, which are intransitive, serve as a link between two words to complete the meaning of a thought. And though they do not take direct objects, they may be completed by a subject complement such as a noun (called a predicate noun or predicate nominative [PN]) or an adjective (called predicate adjective [PA]). Study the following examples to see how linking verbs "link" the subject to their predicate adjectives.

Leaves of maple trees become a beautiful red in the autumn.

S	P(LV)	PA
Leaves	become	red

The verb *become* links *leaves* to *red.* The word *red* is not a DO because it doesn't receive action, but it is an adjective (PA) or complement. Notice the diagonal line.

Cedar-lined closets smell good.

S	P(LV)	PA
closets	smell	good

In the above, the verb *smell* is another linking verb, as are most of the five senses (feel, hear, etc.). So complements are adjectives, or they may be nouns (PNs). And as is the case with PAs, predicate nouns are "linked" to their subjects by the verb. Study these examples:

Maya Angelou is a well-known poet.

S	P(LV)	PN
Maya Angelou	is	poet

Poet is a noun, not an adjective, so it's called the predicate noun, or subject complement. Notice that it's diagrammed the same way as a PA, with the diagonal line between the predicate and the subject complement. Here's another example:

Dale's old blue car was a Chevrolet.

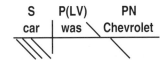

Again, in this example, the word *Chevrolet* is a noun and is therefore called a PN because it's linked to the subject by a linking verb. Therefore, intransitive verbs:

1. do not take direct objects.

2. may or may not have a complement.

3. if there is a complement, can only be an adjective (PA) or a noun (PN).

4. may consist of LVs.

Although linking verbs are good "connectors," they may, however, make writing, or the voice of what's written, passive. We studied voice in the last chapter. So it's best to avoid overusing passive voice when writing or speaking. Notice the difference in voice:

passive: **The bike accident was caused by a broken chain.**
active: **A broken chain caused the bike accident.**

Active voice uses action verbs, or predicates that don't rely on linking verbs or other non-action verbs; however, linking verbs aren't the only kind of predicates that make writing passive. Jaded and overused verbs like *run, talk, come,* do so, too, as do auxiliary (or "helping") verbs such as *has been.* Active voice is nearly always more powerful than passive. The verb form *to be* is linking. By grasping which verbs are linking and auxiliary, you not only know whether the sentence takes a PN or PA, but you also strengthen communication by limiting expression to active voice.

The Most Common "To Be" Verbs and Auxiliary Verbs

be	will be	would be
am	shall be	should be
being	will have been	can be
is	has been	could be
are	have been	should have been
was	had been	would have been
were	shall have been	could have been

smell	taste	look	remain
become	can	may	stay
grow	might	does	do
feel	sound	seem	appear
did			

Thus, linking verbs and auxiliary verbs may act in a passive manner, but not always. Linking verbs can be followed by an adjective and are called predicate adjectives (PA). Passive voice is implied with the word "by," since the action is received by the subject instead of the subject doing the action.

By studying this chart, you can see how linking and auxiliary verbs affect the voice:

	Present	Past	Past Participle
active	drench	drenched	drenched
passive	may drench	has drenched	had drenched
active	praise	praised	praised
passive	can praise	has praised	could have praised
active	go	went	gone
passive	might go	did go	must have gone

In each of the verbs above, the active voice is more powerful while the addition of the auxiliary verb dilutes the voice.

In summary, then, transitive verbs are action verbs that take objects to complete their action, while intransitive verbs don't take objects, though they may have a PN or PA to complete their thought. Linking and auxiliary verbs may make the voice of one's writing passive, so it's best to avoid them.

Verbals

Verbals look like verbs but behave as other parts of speech. There are three major types of verbals: infinitives, participles, and gerunds. They are included in this chapter because of their verb-like appearance. Let's look at each of these.

Infinitives: An infinitive is a "to" verb form, as in *to dance* or *to walk.* A root verb that combines with the "to" form, then, is an infinitive, although sometimes the "to" is understood to be there. This type of verbal may be used in the following ways in a sentence:

A. As nouns: Since infinitives can act as nouns, they can behave as subjects, DOs, and PNs. Let's look at each of these:

1. Subjects: Infinitives can behave as subjects. The diagram model for this is:

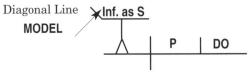

Notice the straight vertical line before the DO.

To play the cello requires talent.

In this case, the root verb, *play,* is preceded by the infinitive *to* which becomes the sentence's subject, and, based on our model, it's diagrammed this way:

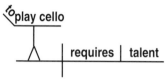

To read requires good light and an eager mind.

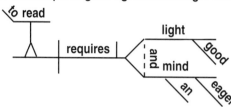

When diagramming infinitives as subjects, they're treated as any other subject of a sentence, meaning they come before the predicate, and are separated by the vertical line.

2. DOs: Since infinitives are nouns, they can also behave as direct objects.

MODEL

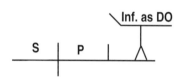

Peter hates to call home.

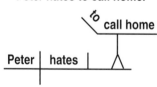

Maggie intended to leave.

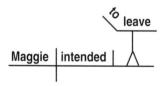

3. PNs: As nouns, infinitives may also act as PNs when there is a linking verb:

MODEL

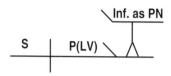

Your duty is to usher theater-goers.

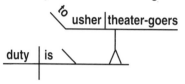

The star of *Hamlet* is to perform tomorrow at the matinee hour.

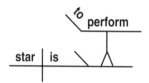

If the DO has an IO, the sentence is diagrammed as any sentence with an indirect object.

B. As adjectives: As adjectives, infinitives can modify nouns or pronouns such as DOs, PNs:

1. Modifying DOs: Infinitives can modify nouns such as DOs.

MODEL

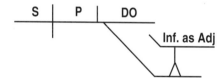

Cory had many things to do.

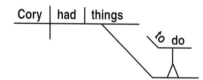

2. Modifying PNs: Since PNs are nouns, infinitives as adjectives can modify them:

MODEL

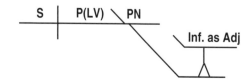

James Baldwin is an author to read.

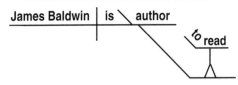

3. Modifying Subjects: As adjectives, infinitives may modify subjects.

MODEL

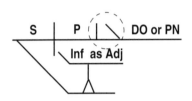

The time to call is Monday morning.

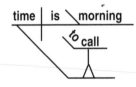

C. As adverbs: Infinitives may function as adverbs modifying verbs, adjectives, and other adverbs.

1. Modifying adjectives: Acting as adverbs, infinitives may modify adjectives.

MODEL

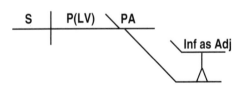

Steadman's ready to go.

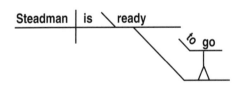

2. Modifying verbs: Infinitives may function as adverbs by modifying the predicate.

MODEL

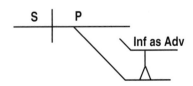

The driver stopped to get directions.

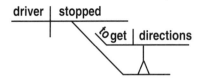

In summary, infinitives are easily recognized verbals by their root verb and *to*. They can function as nouns, adjectives, and adverbs. Their structure consists of a diagonal line joined to a horizontal one and placed on stilts. They may also be found in past tense form, such as *to have been selected*.

Participles: Like infinitives, participles are also verbals, but they behave strictly as adjectives modifying nouns. They come in two forms: the present tense (walk) which combines with the -ing suffix *(walking);* or in the past tense which may be made from the -ed ending to form *walked*. But the past participle of irregular verbs varies. Here's an example:

Sitting next to Jason, Beth felt safe.

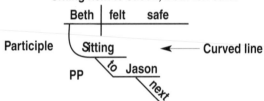

Sitting is a present participle expressed in passive voice modifying the noun *Beth*.

All things considered, Mignon was better off without him.

This is an absolute phrase which really has no tense but is functioning as a noun. *Considered* is a past participle expressed in passive voice. Its participial phrase includes *all things*. Participial phrases are diagrammed next to the nouns they modify, and may be placed on a curved line, though some grammarians prefer a bent horizontal line.

The woman talking to my little sister is her dance teacher.

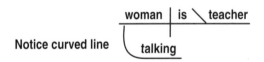

Did you know the man carrying the thick book?

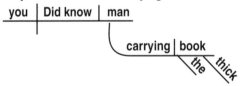

The participial phrase, *carrying the thick book,* which is an adjective, modifies the DO, *man,* which is a noun. As seen in the above example,

participles may also take objects or complements. DOs of participles are diagrammed the same as any DO. Here's an example of a participle combined with an infinitive to modify the DO:

They set up a front to sell stolen electronics.

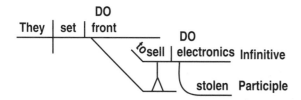

Participles as verbals, then, look like verbs but act like adjectives, and thus modify nouns such as DOs or subjects. They may be placed on curved lines, and when they combine with other words to create a phrase, they're called **participial phrases.** There is a third type of verbal called Gerunds.

Gerunds: Present participles and gerunds look alike since they both end in *-ing,* and so they're sometimes confused. Their difference comes in their use: Participles are used as adjectives, while gerunds are used as nouns; and since they are nouns, they may function as a sentence's subject, object, or object of a preposition.

A. As subjects: Gerunds as subjects behave as the subject in other kinds of sentences.

MODEL

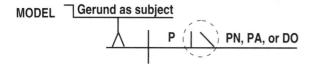

A sentence with a gerund may also have an IO when DOs are present, and the gerund phrase itself may have a complement or object of its own.

Jogging raises the heart rate.

Here, *jogging* is the gerund but it looks like a participle because of its *-ing* ending.

notice the hook joined to a horizontal line, placed on stilts

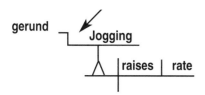

In this example, the present participle form is called the gerund (see previous diagram), because it is used as a noun. It is also used to form the progressive tense as well adjectives.

B. As objects: Just as nouns may serve as DOs or PNs, so may gerunds.
MODEL

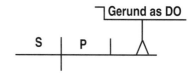

I like listening to classical music.

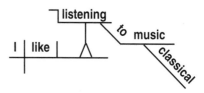

In this example, the gerund phrase, *listening to classical music,* is made up of the root gerund *listening* and its prepositional phrase, all of which serve as the DO. If the sentence has a linking verb, the gerund is a PN and is diagrammed in the same manner.

C. As object of a preposition (OP): Because gerunds are verbals acting as nouns, they can also be objects of prepositions.

MODEL

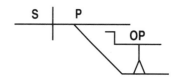

She never talks about acting in her theater company.

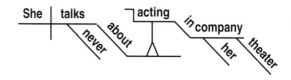

Although gerunds frequently function in present tense in the *-ing* form, they may also behave in past tense. This is an absolute phrase because gerunds function as nouns.

Having been robbed was a frightening experience.

The gerund phrase, *Having been robbed,* is a gerund acting as the subject of a sentence, but instead of being in the present tense form *(-ing),* it's functioning in past tense.

In summary, then, gerunds are verbals acting as nouns that may function as subjects, direct objects, objects of prepositions, appositives, and predicate nominatives. They are recognized by the hooked horizontal line on stilts. See the Review on page 39.

Activities

A. In the following sentences, underline the participle once, the infinitive twice, and circle the gerund.

Example:

With the teacher hovering over him, Burt made mistakes.

1. Fighting is no way to settle a disagreement.
2. He was proud to have been selected for the National Guard.
3. To live happily ever after is everyone's dream.
4. Learning to drive for the first time is frightening.
5. Rebecca fears walking alone at night in the big city.
6. Lenny hates driving in rush hour traffic.
7. All night, Mariette heard her neighbor playing the sax.
8. The plane, buffeted by severe air currents, bounced around enough to cause air sickness in some passengers.
9. Chained to a stake, the Doberman barked for hours.
10. Approaching the street vendor, Helen bought a chili dog.
11. Telling the difference between identical twins isn't easy.
12. Wasn't she going to see her again?

B. Diagram these sentences, and label the parts.

Example:

Seeking answers to questions, John went to the professor's office to ask for help.

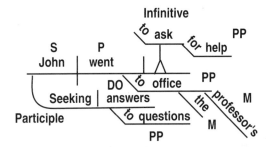

1. To be a best-selling author takes talent and experience.
2. To err is human, and to forgive is divine.
3. Losing her wallet sent Jill into a spin.
4. Dugan's preoccupied with selling crafts.
5. Thinking about the accident upset her.
6. Following her mom's example, she's studying to be a doctor.
7. To study for my literature exam, I need to borrow your book.
8. The supervisor is the one to see about the job.

9. Marie's too sick to go.
10. The music playing around us is too loud for us.
11. Hiking and picking flora are not my "thing."
12. My brother is always looking for ways to sell used cars.
13. The farmer hates to go to the city to sell his products.
14. Blowing out cake candles, the toddler clapped and jumped.
15. Making a mistake is perfectly natural and human.
16. Millie gave Sally her bowling ball.
17. Holding her breath, Meg waited to see the doctor.
18. Intending to sign up for a language, Greg bought a Spanish text.
19. Do you want to go first, or do you want to wait until tomorrow?
20. Swimming is a favorite sport of many teens.
21. Painting pine cones is a fun Christmas craft.
22. Boating on the lake was exciting.

C. Write v.t. over the transitive verb, and v.i. over the intransitive verb.

Example:

   v.t.   v.i.

Pat created a sculpture for a show but it wasn't good enough to win.

1. Krissy covered her ears and hid under the covers as thunder cracked.
2. Will you please hurry?
3. Millicent's reading *A Tale of Two Cities*.
4. Elliot became the first Eagle Scout in his troop.
5. Where does Carmen's sister live?
6. Vince gave Miriam and Chester his baseball card collection.
7. Who's there?
8. The Boston cream pie smells delicious.
9. Remind me to call the doctor tomorrow.
10. She made the chili spicy.
11. List ten qualities of good fiction.
12. Put yourself in his place.
13. Isn't this your second child?
14. Are we alone?
15. I didn't see anything.

Review

1. Intransitive verbs (v.i.) do not take DOs, but all transitive verbs (v.t.) do; some intransitive predicates are action verbs.

2. Linking verbs are v.i. and are passive; they may have complements such as predicate adjectives or predicate nouns.

3. Auxiliary or helping verbs may also make the voice passive.

4. An infinitive is a verbal made up of its main or root verb with *to* present or understood. It may behave as a noun, adjective, or adverb.

5. Participles are verbals with the *-ing* ending when in present tense, and the *-ed* suffix in past tense. When combined with groups of words, they're called participial phrases. Since they behave like adjectives they may modify DOs, Ss, or OPs.

6. Gerunds are a third type of verbal that also has the *-ing* form, but they're used as nouns functioning as subjects, objects, objects of prepositions, or predicate nominatives.

Characteristics of Infinitives

1. verbal with root verb plus *to* (which may be understood)
2. behave as nouns:
   1. subjects
   2. direct objects
   3. predicate nouns (or nominatives)

   adjectives modifying:
   1. subjects
   2. direct objects
   3. predicate nouns

   adverbs modifying:
   1. adjectives
   2. verbs
   3. other adverbs

3. infinitive + modifiers = infinitive phrase

Characteristics of Participles

1. verbals ending in *-ing* form the present particple, and *-ed* forms the past participle
2. behave as adjectives modifying:
   1. subjects
   2. direct objects
   3. objects of prepositions

3. participle + modifiers = participial phrase
4. forms the progressive tense
5. acts as a noun

Characteristics of Gerunds

1. verbal ending in *-ing* form
2. behave as nouns:
   1. subjects
   2. objects
   3. objects of prepositions
   4. appositives
   5. predicate nominatives

3. gerund + modifers = gerund phrase
4. the present participle form used as a noun

CHAPTER 6

This chapter focuses on modifiers, which are words or groups of words that describe, and, in fact, are sometimes called "descriptors." Modifiers are adjectives or adverbs, although sometimes a modifier may act as either, such as the words *little, bad, well,* or *good.* Modifiers help readers mentally create images or pictures of what's being talked about. But their use should be limited to a few powerful ones, as overusing them weakens good writing.

Adjectives

These modifiers tell what kind, how much, or which one. Adjectives modify nouns and pronouns.

Adjectives (examples)

Which one	How Many	What Kind
that	many	huge
this	more	red
those	forty	old
these		wild

Adjectives usually appear before the word they modify: "a deep, purple flower"

The adjectives *deep* and *purple* modify the noun *flower,* and appear before it. But sometimes the adjectives come after the noun for effect or emphasis:

He's a big man, long-legged and broad-shouldered.

Here, the hyphenated adjectives follow the noun *man* to give the description greater stress. In order to use adjectives correctly, it's important to know their comparative forms.

Adjectives in Comparison

Positive Form	Comparative Form	Superlative Form
many	more	most
low	lower	lowest
bad	worse	worst
good	better	best
famous	more famous	most famous
well	better	best
much	more	most

Tangram: The "Chinese Puzzle Game" or Dissection Puzzle swept Europe and America in the early part of the 19th Century. The pieces are 7 shapes cut from a square in a certain way. They can be assembled to form figures of people, animals and everyday objects, as well as geometrical shapes, numbers and letters. It later became known as "Tangram."

Notice in the comparison chart, how some of the forms change, such as *bad, good, famous, well, much.* The comparative form contrasts two things, while the superlative compares more than two. Be careful not to use double comparatives or superlatives, such as:

more faster   most happiest   more quicker   most eeriest

This would be incorrect or substandard grammar. Equally wrong is forming a comparative or superlative with an "incomparable adjective":

deadest   uniquest   perfecter   emptier

If something is "dead," it can't be any "deader" or "deadest." There are no comparisons for such words as above, so be on guard when using adjectives. There are six major types of adjectives, some of which cross over into other parts of speech:

1. Possessive pronouns: These are adjectives that show ownership:

   my   their   your

2. Articles: These adjectives are also called "determiners."

   a   an   the

3. Relative pronouns: Sometimes these are understood and, hence, are not written. The word *that* is the most common but others include *which, who,* and so on.

4. Demonstrative pronouns: These indicate distance:

   this   these   that   those

5. Personal pronouns: Like possessive pronouns, these show ownership:

   my   his

6. Proper adjectives: These are derived from proper nouns and are capitalized:

   Italian currency   Doberman pincer   Oriental rug

41

When diagramming adjectives, place them on a diagonal line under the word they modify:

The olden times of yesteryear were better.

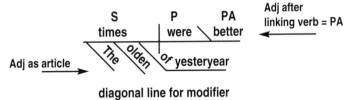

diagonal line for modifier

The Baltimore Orioles are red birds, and a Maryland baseball team.

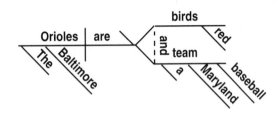

Count the adjectives: *the* is an article and an adjective, *Baltimore* and *Maryland* are proper adjectives, *red* and *baseball* are common adjectives.

The rickety, old truck collided with a lawn mower.

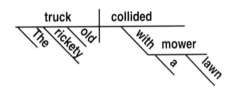

In summary, then, adjectives tell which one, how many, and what kind, and can be made of different types, such as personal or relative pronouns. Adjectives modify nouns and pronouns, and they're similar to the adverb.

Adverbs

These modifiers or descriptors qualify verbs, adjectives, and other adverbs. They tell how, where, when, and to what extent.

Adverbs (examples)

How	Where	When	To what extent
rapidly	above	now	slowly, rarely, briefly
sadly	farther	later	frequently
happily	there	afterwards	lightly
earnestly	nearby	lastly	always
eagerly	here	then	often, cautiously
angrily	upstairs	before	never

Many adverbs end in **-ly,** but some don't and so they may be confused with adjectives. Just

42

remember that adverbs are limited to modifying verbs, adverbs, and adjectives.

adverb:	She drives carefully.
adjective:	She is a careful driver.

In the first example, the **-ly** ending makes the word an adverb modifying the verb, whereas in the second sentence, *careful* is used as an adjective modifying the noun *driver*. Notice, that as is true with adjectives, adverbs are generally placed next to the word they modify. And also like adjectives, adverbs can be used in comparison.

Adverbs in Comparison

Positive Form	Comparative Form	Superlative Form
early	earlier	earliest
well	better	best
clearly	more clearly	most clearly
fast	faster	fastest
soon	sooner	soonest
badly	worse	worst
little	less	least

Some words may function as adverbs or prepositions (see Chapter Seven), depending on how they're used:

Adverb	Preposition
1. She dared to leap across.	1. He traveled across the state.
2. He set the milk bottle down.	2. She ran down the hospital hall.
3. The stew boiled over.	3. She drove over the icy roads.
4. The dog turned around.	4. She ran around the corner.
5. Attorney Cooper is in.	5. The relish is in the refrigerator.

Always study how a word is used in context to determine if it's an adjective, adverb, or preposition, but generally adverbs are easy to recognize, and for that reason, they're just as easy to diagram. They're placed on a diagonal line underneath the word they modify.

MODEL

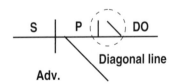

Electricity is conducted easily through water.

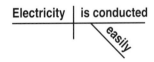

Notice how the adverb, *easily,* is placed underneath the verb. Here's another example:

Benny will go there tomorrow after school.

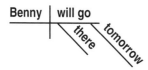

In the above example, there is a double adverb, both modifying the verb, as is true for this next example:

Dick hardly worked hard.

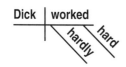

Adverbs may also appear with verbs that take objects:

The expectant father anxiously paced the waiting room.

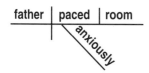

The toddlers danced eagerly and frenetically to the Irish Jig.

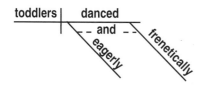

Notice the adverbs joined by the word *and*, a conjunction.

Sometimes, in speech and writing, we mix up the order of words, misplacing the modifiers. Below, the word *immediately* is confusing as to whether it modifies *job* or *developed*.

To get the job immediately Robert developed a resume.

Would this work better?

To get the job, Robert immediately developed a resume.

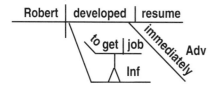

It's important when using modifiers to make sure their meaning is clear and precise.

Just as there are different types of adjectives, so are there categories of adverbs, some which cross over and may be used in more than one way. These categories consist of:

1. Conjunctive adverbs: These are adverbs that connect one idea to another:

in addition	in fact	naturally	unfortunately
thus	nevertheless	so	then
consequently	therefore	meanwhile	obviously
apparently	perhaps	moreover	instead
hence	besides	also	however

2. Absolute adverbs: they are like limiting or absolute adjectives in that they don't have degrees of comparison.

perfectly	straightly	dead	impossibly
round	uniquely	infinitively	

3. Relative pronouns: These were discussed under adjectives, and include:

that	whom	whomever	whoever
which	who	whose	

Adjective and Adverb Phrases and Clauses

When a modifier is accompanied by another word or group of words, it's called a phrase. Both adjectives and adverbs may form phrases or clauses (clauses have a subject and a verb, whereas phrases don't). Like singular adjectives, adjective phrases modify nouns and pronouns, and adverb phrases describe verbs, adverbs, and adjectives. Although clauses are introduced here, they are discussed more fully in Chapter Eight.

Example:

Tired and dirty, the football player trudged back to the locker room.

Tired and dirty, functions as an adjective modifying the noun *player.* Clauses may also rely on conjunctions and pronouns, as in this example:

The panelist who's talking is president of a college.

Who's talking behaves as an adjective modifying *panelist*. And the word *who* (see box on previous page) is a relative pronoun. This sentence would be diagrammed this way:

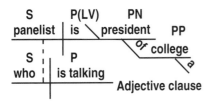

Here's another example: "Won't you answer the questions that I asked you?"

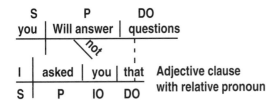

The clause, *that I asked you* is an adjective modifying the direct object, *questions*.

Adverb clauses behave like adjective clauses, but unlike adjective clauses which appear near the word they modify, adverb clauses can appear anywhere in a sentence. Study these examples:

Andrew runs faster than I do.

The clause *than I do,* modifies the word *faster,* which is an adverb, and since adverbs or adverbial clauses and phrases modify other adverbs, verbs, and adjectives, it would be diagrammed this way:

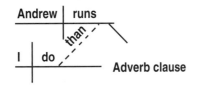

If Bobby knocks really hard, let him in.

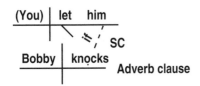

In the above example, the SC, *if,* connects the two clauses. Chapter Seven details conjunctions. But notice how conjunctions serve to "connect" one clause or phrase to another. Subordinating conjunctions (SC) are used with adverb clauses and are the most abundant of all the conjunctions.

44

Some subordinating conjunctions also function as prepositions. Here's a list:

after	if	because	before	than
although	as if	as long as	as soon as	as far as
as though	than	in order that	so that	where
whenever	since	whenever	though	whether
while	unless	wherever	until	when

SCs reduce the clause to one of dependency, making it subordinate or reliant on the independent clause, as in:

Before a tornado hits, a loud rumbling can be heard.

The subordinating conjunction, *before,* makes the adverb clause, *a tornado hits,* dependent on *a loud rumbling can be heard.* Without the independent clause, *a loud rumbling can be heard,* the adverb clause makes no sense, and thus becomes an incomplete sentence or fragment.

To learn whether a phrase or clause is an adjective or adverb, it's a good idea to associate which conjunctions and pronouns go with which modifiers.

Activities

A. In the following paragraph, write C if the numbered modifier is used correctly, but write the proper modifier in the blank if it's not.

example   1
Whitney looked *loving* at her kitty named Beau. He had greenly
                          2
colored eyes that shone bright in the dark. She picked him up
                  3
and held him tight to her chest, cooing at him. She whispered,
                                                                  4
"Oh, Beau, I love you so much. Will you always be my precious
                          5
kitty?" She lowered him gently to the ground and watched him
          6
happily scamper through the house. When she next looked at
                                  7
him, he seemed more happy than when she had last held him.
              8
She gladly poured more food into his dish because she loved
          9   10
happy, fattest cats. She was even thinking about buying a more
      11   12
fatter kitty, making him happier than Beau.

Example: **lovingly**

1._____	7._____
2._____	8._____
3._____	9._____
4._____	10._____
5._____	11._____
6._____	12._____

B. Write T for true and F for false:

Example:

Adverb phrases have a subject and a predicate.　　　　　**F**

1. Adjectives modify nouns and predicates. ____
2. Adjectives have no superlative degree. ____
3. Adverbs modify verbs, adverbs, and adjectives. ____
4. Both adverbs and adjectives have a positive and comparative form. ____
5. Many adverbs end in -ly. ____
6. The word *before* is an absolute adverb. ____
7. Adjectives modify phrases and clauses. ____
8. This sentence is correct: "He looked differently to his father." ____
9. This is incorrect: "Thinking about her mom's death, she felt bad." ____

C. Underline the clause or phrase in each sentence, and write in the blank *Adj* if it's an adjective, or *Adv* if it's an adverb.

Example:

When I received the flowers, I cried loudly.　　　**adv**

1. As long as I'm in charge, changes will be made. ____
2. You must go before the teacher arrives. ____
3. Uncle Bob, who is my mother's brother, will visit tomorrow. ____
4. The motorist who stopped to change our tire is a relative. ____
5. I'll dial the number if you'll talk to her. ____
6. The movie he scripted will be on television next year. ____
7. The little girl who had come to our door was selling Girl Scout cookies. ____
8. Give the teacher some reason why you missed her class. ____
9. Hollan didn't go to church because he had the flu. ____
10. I'll read the directions after I remove all the parts from the box. ____

D. In each sentence below, write in the blank whether the word next to the verb is an adjective or adverb, and then diagram the framework to include any modifiers.

Example:

She looked exhausted.　　　　　　　**exhausted, PA**

　　　She | looked \ exhausted

1. Barbara is well. ____
2. He dances well. ____
3. Everything seems blurry with my new glasses. ____
4. The prisoner's cell looked neat. ____
5. The no-bake, chocolate cookies were absolutely magnificent. ____
6. Wesley and Rick diligently worked on their lab report. ____
7. Delia and Millie are reliable babysitters and serious students. ____
8. It is finished. ____
9. They call me Mr. Tibbs. ____
10. They will never go for your idea. ____
11. She loudly announced the news. ____
12. She usually writes romance novels. ____
13. Never call me. ____
14. Yesterday Leif sent her a colorful photo. ____
15. Reuben quit. ____

E. Diagram each sentence and label the sentence parts; identify clauses.

Example:

The woman who's standing on the stage behind the lectern is the mayor of the city.

　　woman | is \ mayor
　　who | is standing

1. Before you buy that car, look at the price.
2. The Victorian house I always wanted was too expensive. (The word *that* is understood.)
3. Mrs. Fowler is the real estate agent from whom my husband and I purchased our house.
4. If you wait, I'll meet you.
5. He washed the floor because he spilled syrup on it.

45

6. When the bell rings, go to algebra class.

7. "The Raven," which Poe wrote, is very scary.

8. The bully who kicked me during recess never liked me.

9. She's a teacher whom I had in third grade.

F. Fill in the chart below for the following modifiers according to their degree.

Adjectives

	Positive	Comparative	Superlative
Example:	little	less	least
1.	good	_____	best
2.	much	more	_____
3.	cold	_____	_____
4.	quick	_____	_____
5.	high	higher	_____
6.	bad	_____	_____

Adverbs

	Positive	Comparative	Superlative
Example:	well	better	best
1.	_____	worse	_____
2.	angrily	_____	_____
3.	_____	sooner	_____
4.	well	_____	_____
5.	jealously	_____	_____
6.	_____	colder	_____

1. Modifiers may be only one word or may be a group of words called a phrase or a clause.

2. Modifiers help readers create pictures or images in their minds.

3. Modifiers need to be placed in proper order to give clear meaning.

4. Adjectives qualify nouns and pronouns, and usually appear before the word they describe.

5. There are different types of adjectives: articles, relative pronouns, possessive pronouns, demonstrative pronouns, proper adjectives.

6. An adjective following a linking verb is called a predicate adjective.

7. Adjectives tell which one, how many, and what kind.

8. Adverbs modify other adverbs, verbs, and adjectives; some adverbs can be made by adding -ly to the adjective form. Adverbs tell how, where, when, and to what extent.

9. Adjectives and adverbs have degrees of comparison; they may also be clauses and phrases.

10. There are different types of adverbs: conjunctive adverbs, absolute adverbs, and relative adverbs

Differences between Adjectives and Adverbs

Adjectives
1. modifies nouns and pronouns
2. different types: possessive
                        demonstrative
                        articles
                        relative
                        personal
3. modify phrases
4. tell: which one
             how many
             what kind
5. have degrees of comparison:
             positive
             comparative
             superlative
6. not always easy to identify

Adverbs
1. modifies verbs, adjectives, and adverbs
2. different types: conjunctive adverbs
                        absolute
                        subordinate
                        relative
3. modify clauses
4. tell: how   when
             where   why
             to what extent
5. have degrees of comparison:
             positive
             comparative
             superlative
6. easy to identify when in -ly form

Review Test 3

I. Underline v.t. once, v.i. twice. After each sentence, write P if its voice is passive, and A if it's active; Circle all linking and auxiliary verbs.

Example:

Generic drugs <u>substitute</u> for brand names.   **A**

1. The explosives have been activated by the demolition team. _____
2. The vase was broken by the twin brothers. _____
3. He broke out into a rash. _____
4. She designs high-tech musical equipment. _____
5. The raging "nor'easter" cancelled the festival. _____
6. Coordinating conjunctions may link independent clauses. _____
7. Eat five vegetables and fruits a day to maintain good health. _____
8. The window panes have been washed by Karen. _____
9. Although salt adds flavor to food, it can lead to heart problems. _____
10. Do you think before you speak? _____
11. Johnson & Johnson, Proctor & Gamble, and Coca-Cola are major advertisers. _____
12. It's by far better to give than to receive. _____
13. Jogging early in the morning is safer than running in afternoon heat. _____
14. Writing lab reports frightens many students. _____

II. Label the sentence parts.

Example:

         Adj   **S(N)**   **P(V)**   **PP**
Generic drugs substitute for brand names.

1. The explosives have been activated by the demolition team.
2. The vase was broken by the twin brothers.
3. He broke out into a rash.
4. She designs high-tech musical equipment.
5. The raging "nor'easter" cancelled the festival.
6. Coordinating conjunctions may link independent clauses.
7. Eat five vegetables and fruits a day to maintain good health.
8. The window panes have been washed by Karen.
9. Although salt adds flavor to food, it can lead to heart problems.
10. Do you think before you speak?
11. Johnson & Johnson, Proctor & Gamble, and Coca-Cola are major advertisers.
12. It's by far better to give than to receive.
13. Jogging early in the morning is safer than running in afternoon heat.
14. Writing lab reports frightens many students.

III. Diagram the following sentences.

Example:

Generic drugs substitute for brand names.

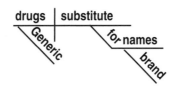

1. Call the 800 number for information.
2. The wind is gusting to thirty-three mph.
3. He broke out into a rash.
4. She designs high-tech musical equipment.
5. Eat five vegetables and fruits.
6. Just say it.
7. Do you think before you speak?
8. Johnson & Johnson, Proctor & Gamble, and Coca-Cola are major advertisers.
9. Greenpeace opposes any type of environmental pollution.
10. Did you have Mrs. Gordon for Algebra I?
11. Ariel likes to ride her bike to school.

IV. Fill in the chart according to degree and identify the type of modifier it is.

	Positive	Comparative	Superlative	Type
Example:	many	more	most	Adj
1.	high			
2.		better		
3.			least	
4.		more happily		
5.	agreeable			
6.		less		
7.	happy	happier		
8.		more bravely		
9.	bad			
10.	soon			
11.	good			
12.	well			

48

V. Correct the mistakes in the following sentences.

Example:

Bob wrote more faster than Harry.

Correct:

Bob | wrote \ faster than Harry

1. The uniquest thing about silk flowers is their durability.
2. There books were stolen from there lockers.
3. You're cup is emptier then mine.
4. Twelve homely guys biked thru the park.
5.

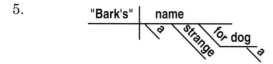

6.

do it

If you | decide | Λ

7.

He | didn't go | nowhere

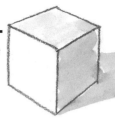

In preceding chapters, verbals (gerunds, infinitives, and participles) were discussed, as well phrases and clauses. This chapter looks at prepositions and prepositional phrases, the various types of conjunctions, along with such special items as appositives, nouns of address, expletives, and interjections.

Prepositions and their Phrases

Prepositions are words that connect one word to another to give color to a thought. While a sentence like "The policeman stopped the car" is adequate and grammatically correct, it, however, doesn't give enough information or provide a good picture. But "connectors" such as prepositions provide details about location, time, kind, and other types of relationships. Compare:

Without prepositions:	The policeman stopped the car.
With prepositions:	The policeman from Dade County stopped the car with the white and red racing stripes, within city limits, around one in the afternoon.

In the second example, the prepositional phrase (PP) *from Dade County* details "where" the officer is from; the prepositional phrase *with the red and white racing stripes* identifies the car or tells what kind; the prepositional phrase *within the city limits* also tells "where" or gives location, while the last phrase, *around one in the afternoon*, tells time. Notice how much more colorful this description is than the first one. From the second example, it can be seen that such words as *from, with, within, around* are prepositions that create PP. The prepositions in the above example link one word to another, and so they serve as connectors. Prepositions also may function as adverbs (see next column), and the only way to determine this is to study how they're used in a sentence. A point to keep in mind is that if the preposition appears alone in the sentence (without a phrase), it's probably an adverb.

Bobby set his lunch down.

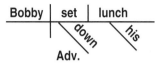

Down has no phrase; how it's used in the sentence indicates it's an adverb, as compared to:

Bobby ran down the football field.

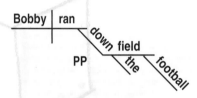

The phrase *down the football field* is anchored to the word *down* which acts like a preposition. Also notice how the two sentences above are diagrammed. In the first example, *down* is placed under the verb *set* because it's an adverb, while in the second example, *down* is fixed to a diagonal line from which its phrase is attached because it's a preposition. Here are some of the common prepositions, which may be used as other parts of speech:

Prepositions

after	along	aside from	along with
against	about	according to	except for
since	except	through	across
till	ahead of	in case of	to
inside	as	as well as	into
toward	as a result of	in connection with	among
in addition to	under	around	in back of
underneath	at	in front of	until
because of	unlike	at the expense of	up
in place of	before	in spite of	upon
behind	inside of	with	below
instead of	with regard to	within	beneath
in view of	like	without	beside
near	considering	besides	of
beyond	on account of	on	on behalf of
but (except)	onto	prior to	by

Prepositions may be used idiomatically—meaning as slang, or not in standard English form:

put up with	put down	in a tiz
make do	put on	take up

LaToya had to put up with her little brother.

A.J. was in a tiz over missing his math exam.

Clichés may be formed by prepositions. It's advisable to avoid them because they're so overused that they no longer create vivid imagery. Here are some prepositions used in clichés:

young in spirit   cool as a cucumber
off the deep end   water under the bridge
other side of the coin   two peas in a pod
on the other hand   rotten to the core
walking on air

Prepositions can function as adjectives modifying nouns or pronouns, and, hence, in a diagram they're placed under the word they describe:

Seanna is the girl in the taffeta dress.

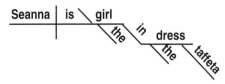

The preposition *in* anchors its phrase *the taffeta dress* to the noun *girl.* Prepositions are placed on diagonal lines underneath the words they modify, with their objects (the object of the preposition [OP]). From this framework, the remaining words in the phrase are attached. Prepositions may also act as adverbs, and thus will modify verbs, adverbs, and adjectives.

The band marched past the judge's stand.

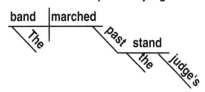

The preposition *past* and its phrase modifies the verb *marched,* and so it's diagrammed on a diagonal line underneath the predicate. If the PP, *the judge's stand,* had been omitted, the word *past* would have acted as an adverb and not a preposition anchoring a phrase. Here's another example of a PP behaving as an adverb:

He docked his boat in the harbor slip.

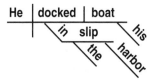

The PP, *in the harbor slip,* tells where, and so it modifies the predicate, and thus is diagrammed underneath the verb, *docked.* Prepositions and their phrases, then, serve to add color to sentences to create imagery, while providing additional information on location, time, and kind. They may also function as adverbs and adjectives.

Conjunctions

Like prepositions, conjunctions connect one word or group of words to another. Of all the parts of speech, these are the least confusing, although some may act as prepositions. But conjunctions, unlike prepositions, don't have objects, so this is one way to tell the difference between them. There are three major types of conjunctions, although similar "connectors" (relative pronouns, conjunctive adverbs) may also be categorized as conjunctions. These similar types were discussed in the last chapter but are presented here again for comparison.

Relative Pronouns

whatever	which	that	whoever
whomever	what	whose	whom

Relative pronouns act as conjunctions as they, too, join one clause to another. They're similar to conjunctive adverbs in that they also connect clauses.

Conjunctive Adverbs

therefore	although	however	nevertheless	also
otherwise	likewise	similarly	furthermore	yet
indeed	meanwhile	besides	moreover	so

Subordinating conjunctions (SC) were mentioned in the last chapter. These connectors introduce dependent or subordinate clauses, which are clauses that can't stand alone in a sentence, meaning they're depending on or relying on another clause to make their meaning clear. The SC, then, links these dependent clauses to the main or independent clause (one that can stand on its own). Below, the SC, *while,* joins the dependent clause to the main one.

subordinate clause   independent clause
  SC
**While Alisa was an exchange student in Italy,
she visited La Scala.**

Sample Subordinating Conjunctions

after	although	as	as long as	as if
as though	in order that	if only	now that	once
since	rather than	so that	whenever	than
that	whereas	while	though	till
unless	provided	until	when	whatever
where	wherever	whether	provided that	as soon as

Clauses with SCs are diagrammed the same way adverb clauses are:

SC
Unless I ask, I'll never know.

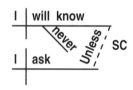

Subordinating conjunctions express the following kinds of relationships:

Use of Subordinating Conjunctions

Relationship	SCs	Example
Time	after, as long as, before, once, as soon as, until, when, while, since, whenever	"After you get there, call me."
Purpose or reason	because, so that, in order that, for, as	"I read that book on karate so that I can protect myself."
Effect	as if, now that, as long as, so	"It's as if he doesn't care anymore."
Condition	provided that, even though, rather than, even if, if, unless,	"We'll go on vacation, provided that it's not hot out."
Comparison	than, although, though	"She's thinner this year than last year."
Place	where, wherever rather, whether	"Wherever she speaks, she gets a standing ovation."

Similar to SCs are coordinating conjunctions (CC) which link like parts of sentences, such as compound subjects, compound predicates, compound phrases and even compound independent clauses:

CC
John and I left for class. (compound subject)

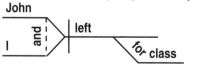

CC
You may walk or run. (compound verb)

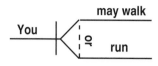

Coordinating Conjunctions

and	nor	yet	but	or	for	so

Correlative conjunctions (CrC) work in pairs to connect like sentence structures. They're similar to CCs.

Correlative Conjunctions (Pairs)

neither...nor	either...or	both...and	not only...but also
not...but	whether...or	as...as	

CrCs are easy to identify since they exist in pairs. Here's how they're diagrammed:

Either Heather or Wendy will audition today.

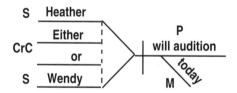

Conjunctions, then, are connectors that complete thoughts while joining one idea to another. There are five different types of conjunctions, with SCs, CCs, and CrCs being the most common.

Special Items

In speech, little thought is given to common expressions or phrases, but in writing or diagramming, they're handled differently. These familiar grammatical items include interjections, expletives, nouns of address, and appositives.

Interjections express feelings or emotions. They command attention, or convey surprise, but have no relationship to other words in a sentence.

Sample Interjections

No!	Gosh!	Help!	Oh!	Listen!	Hey!
Yipes!	Wow!	Alas!	Quick!	Holy cow!	Golly!
Hooray!	Wait!	Watch it!	Great!	Ouch!	Goodness!

When used alone, interjections are punctuated with an exclamation point, but when used in a sentence, or expressing only a mild emotion, the exclamation mark is replaced with a comma:

Used alone: "Ouch! That hurt."
Within sentence: "No, I didn't go."

Interjections are diagrammed this way: "Wow! Isn't she beautiful."

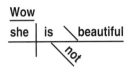

Expletives have no function in grammar other than to serve as fillers, so they often blur the meaning of sentences and weaken their impact. Rewrite sentences when expletives are overused.

Expl
There are many kinds of computers available that advance home businesses.

Better:

Businesses in the home can be advanced by the different computers available.

Since an expletive doesn't modify anything, it's diagrammed on a line by itself:

Expl
There was a big bear.

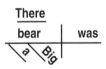

Expl
It was a dark and stormy night.

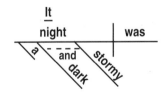

Don't confuse expletives with introductory words that modify a part of speech, such as verbs:

Here they are.

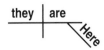

54

Where have you been?

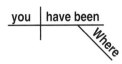

Like expletives, Nouns of Address don't modify anything, and, hence, are set aside in a diagram. In writing, they're separated by a comma.

Joe, come now.

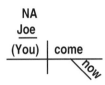

Notice how *Joe* is the noun being addressed, and is separated from the rest of the sentence by a comma. Also, it's diagrammed similarly to an expletive. Here's another example:

Yes, Virginia, there is a Santa Claus.

An Appositive is yet another grammatical construction that isn't part of a sentence. This type of expression explains, renames, or identifies some other word. Appositives may be restrictive or non-restrictive. Restrictive appositives are an integral part of a sentence, meaning they can't be omitted without confusing the meaning, but non-restrictive appositives can be omitted.

Restrictive
The initial 'F' in President John F. Kennedy's name comes from his mother's surname.

In this case, the appositive, *F*, is restrictive because without it, the sentence would be confusing; notice how it's diagrammed:

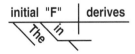

However, in the next example, the appositive could be omitted without damaging the intent of the sentence:

Nonrestrictive
The class nominated my enemy, Dawn, for president.

The name *Dawn* is not restrictive because the sentence would still make sense without it. The inclusion of the name gives added clarity but it's not integral to the meaning. Nonrestrictive appositives are diagrammed like this:

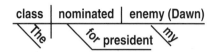

Notice how nonrestrictive appositives are placed in parentheses next to the nouns they modify.

In summary, special grammatical items add to the meaning of sentences, but, except for a few, they are not vital to the structure, and, hence, are set apart by commas, or are placed on separate lines when diagrammed.

Activities

A. Underline all PPs once, double underline the OP, circle prepositions acting as adverbs, place a box around those that are idiomatic in clichés, and triple underline appositives.

Example:

Under the dark green sea, there exist plants and animals of various shapes and colors.

Example:

Breck looked around the class after he did a "cut up" on Sam in front of everyone.

1. Observers shouldn't view solar eclipses without the aid of specially designed glasses.
2. She owns the McDonalds at Fifth and Main Streets.
3. Our dog, Cinco, smells of the outside.
4. Poems about love seem to carry a special music of their own.
5. Joanna was embarrassed by the put-down.
6. Beneath the eaves of the roof stands an old man with a cane.
7. Tell me no lies.
8. The veterans of the Vietnam War marched past the Statue of Liberty.
9. Harriet was out of her league in the State Science Competition.
10. Mrs. Ramsay, the school principal, laid down the law.

B. Underline any conjunctions.

Example:

Either Gaby's going to babysit, or Peggy is.

1. She ate four slices of pizza and drank two glasses of Pepsi.
2. Marti still works for the Saks Fifth Avenue Company that she started with ten years ago.
3. While Donnie was playing football, he also practiced for basketball.
4. I didn't want to go because there would be too many people there.
5. He studied linguistics intensely, so he should know word derivations.
6. Whoever arrives first will have to help me with decorations.
7. Bobbette is taller than she.
8. You may talk quietly or read books.
9. Cramer was tired and exhausted.
10. He asked not only once, but also twice.

C. Diagram the following sentences, but do not diagram any clauses except those that are verbals.

Example:
S   PP   P   Inf   M   M   Obj of Inf PP
Poems about love seem to carry a special music of their own.

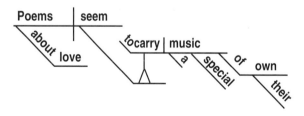

1. Neither Gabe nor Becca enjoyed the dinner.
2. Well, goodness gracious, Jackie! I haven't seen you in years.
3. I bought a ticket, but I really didn't want to go.
4. Breck looked around.
5. Jack, did you ask a question?
6. Hurrah! Our team won the finals.
7. Of course I did all the math.
8. I put her feathered cap there.
9. Help! I can't hold the box anymore.
10. It was difficult to understand him.

Review

1. Prepositions provide detail and color to a sentence while acting as links or connections.

2. Besides acting as "connectors," prepositions also may function as other POS in a sentence, such as adverbs.

3. Prepositions may be used idiomatically in clichés, such as "walking on air."

4. Like prepositions, conjunctions behave as connectors.

5. There are three major classes of conjunctions, but there are really five types:

   1. subordinating conjunctions   4. relative pronouns
   2. correlative conjunctions   5. conjunctive adverbs
   3. coordinating conjunctions

6. Relative pronouns are conjunctions that introduce and link subordinate clauses to their independent clause. Because they connect a subordinate clause, they're sometimes labeled as "subordinating conjunctions."

7. Conjunctive adverbs act like conjunctions in that they join clauses in sentences.

8. Subordinating conjunctions introduce dependent or subordinate clauses and link them to independent clauses. They're diagrammed the same way as adverb clauses.

9. Coordinating conjunctions, which are few in number, link like parts of sentences which result in the formation of compound structures (compound subjects, compound predicates, compound phrases, compound dependent clauses, compound sentences).

10. Correlative conjunctions work in pairs to join sentence parts.

11. Expletives are fillers in a sentence, and are placed on a separate line in diagrams.

12. Interjections express emotions, but have no relationship to other parts of a sentence.

13. Nouns of address name the person who is being addressed, and are separated by a comma from the rest of the sentence.

14. Appositives explain, rename, or identify some other word, and they may be restrictive or nonrestrictive.

Although clauses and phrases have been discussed in other sections, this chapter will not only serve as review, but it will also function as an introduction to other types of clauses and their various complex constructions. Besides the verbals so far looked at, which sometimes appear as phrases, this section also delves into noun, adjective, and adverb clauses.

Review of Verbals

Verbals (infinitives, gerunds, and participles) are POS that look like verbs but function in some other manner. When verbals are accompanied by modifiers or objects, they form phrases.

Infinitives may be preceded by *to;* they function as nouns, adverbs, or adjectives.

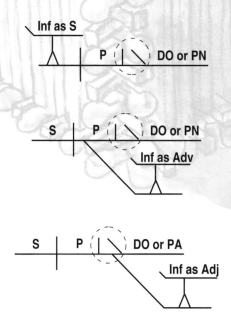

Gerunds (*-ing* ending) act as nouns and function as S, PN, DO, AP, OP.

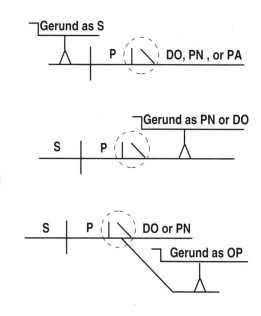

As appositives, gerunds may take one of the forms above.

Participles also may end in *-ing,* as well as other suffixes, and may function as adjectives modifying nouns or pronouns; also participles may appear in present or past form.

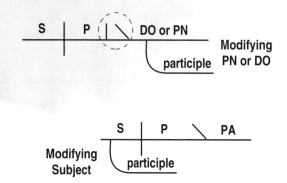

Prepositional Phrases, which have already been discussed, are another type of phrase which may function as adjective or adverb.

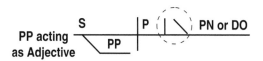

Matchstick Puzzle: With the invention of matches came matchstick puzzles as 3-dimensional objects and as puzzles. Nothing holds the 114 matchsticks of this structure together except the ingenuity of its design. The first part of the building is log-cabin technique: One 4-match square piled on top of another.

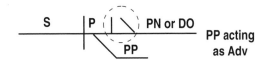

PP acting
as Adv

Having reviewed phrases, the remainder of this chapter will now concentrate on clauses: adverb, adjective, and noun. A characteristic of clauses is that they contain both a subject and a verb. They may be independent or dependent.

Clauses: Subject + Predicate
1. Independent: Complete thought; can stand alone; may act as main clause, "She watches the Discovery Channel."
2. Dependent: Incomplete thought; not a sentence; relies on main clause, "After he visited her."

Dependent clauses may function as:
A. Adverbs = modify verbs, adjectives, adverbs: "As soon as he came, he left."
B. Adjectives = modify nouns, pronouns: "I saw my boss who is the principal."
C. Nouns = don't modify anything; fulfill noun functions: "I see that you're taller than your sister."

Let's look at each of these three types of dependent clauses in detail:

A. Adverb Clauses: These dependent structures contain a subject and predicate, and are usually followed by a comma. But because they are dependent, they rely on independent clauses to complete their meaning. Adverb clauses behave like adverbs, in that they modify verbs, adjectives, and other adverbs. They rely on subordinating conjunctions (SCs) to connect them to the main clause, but they also may be introduced by relative pronouns.

SC
When he drove my car, I got nervous.

The SC, *when,* connects the adverb clause to the main one. This could also read: "I got nervous when he drove my car." Adverbial clauses give information on time, place or location, manner, condition, cause, purpose or reason, comparison or degree, how much, concession, when, how often. These types of clauses form complex sentences.

1. Modifying verbs:

MODEL

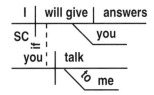

If you talk to me, I'll give you answers.

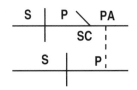

adverb clause modifying verb

2. Modifying adjectives:

MODEL

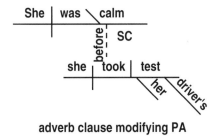

adverb clause modifying predicate adjective

She was calm before she took her driver's test.

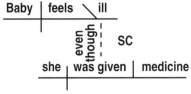

adverb clause modifying PA

Baby feels ill even though she was given medicine.

adverb clause modifying adjective

3. Modifying adverbs:

MODEL

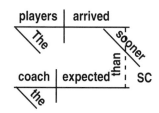

The players arrived sooner than the coach expected.

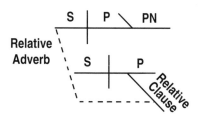

adverb clause modifying adverb

B. Adjective clauses are dependent clauses that act like adjectives, and thus modify nouns and pronouns. Relative pronouns (that, whoever, whom, etc.) and relative adverbs (where, when, why) introduce adjective clauses, although the relative pronoun is often understood, and, hence, not written. While the relative adverb acts as an adverb, the relative pronouns may serve as DOs, IOs, OPs, or Ss. Here are some examples:

1. Adjective clauses with relative adverbs:

MODEL

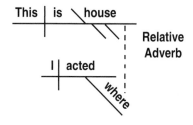

This is the theater house where I acted.

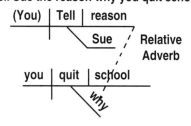

Tell Sue the reason why you quit school.

2. Adjective clauses with relative pronouns:

MODEL

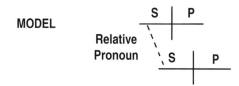

Relative pronoun as subject:

Cronkite is the reporter who's well-known.

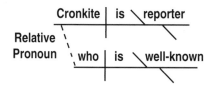

Relative pronoun as object of preposition:

The Davenports are the neighbors with whom I visited.

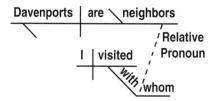

Relative pronoun as indirect object:

OP
The teacher to whom I spoke explained your grades.

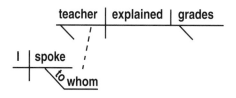

As direct objects:

OP
Children are the group of people with whom I visit.

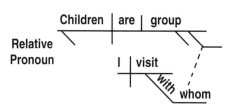

C. Noun clauses are subordinates that function in a sentence as any noun would: as DO, OP, S, PN, IO, AP. Since noun clauses aren't modifiers, they can't qualify or describe any POS, but they can substitute for a noun in a sentence. Noun clauses are recognized by their "connectors" which include SC, and some relative pronouns. These connectors include:

whoever	whomever	whose	when	that
whatever	whether	what	whom	why
who	where	how	if	

Noun clauses fall into one of these patterns:

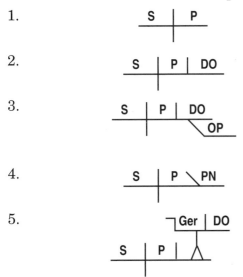

1. As subjects:

What he said angered me.

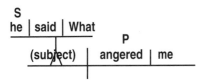

2. As direct objects:

I know who will sing next.

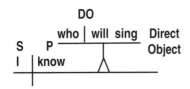

3. As objects of prepositions:

Antonia cried over what she had seen.

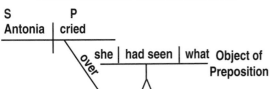

4. As predicate nominatives:

Julian is whom we want.

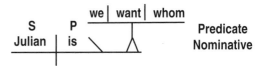

5. As indirect object:

Give whoever asks the list of books.

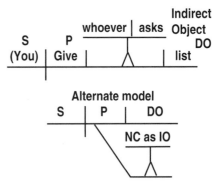

In conclusion, each clause is diagrammed a particular way, depending on how it's used in a sentence, and what type of conjunction joins it to the independent clause. Phrases and clauses, such as verbals, prepositions, adverbs, adjectives, and nouns, give additional information while adding color to a sentence. Because clauses are like sentences within sentences, they can become complicated, especially with the addition of prepositional phrases. Below are samples of **complex,** and **compound-complex** sentences.

Advanced Diagramming

Simple sentences have only one subject and one predicate. But some simple sentences may have compound subjects (two or more) or compound predicates. However, if one independent clause is joined to another independent clause, it becomes a **compound sentence.** Compound sentences require a coordinating conjunction to connect them, such as this:

My sister and I love and adore pets, and we'll do anything for them.

compound subject   compound predicate

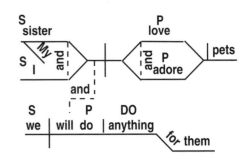

By adding dependent clauses, such as noun, adjective, or adverb clauses, as well as verbals and prepositional phrases, a sentence can be made **compound-complex,** like this:

My sister and I unequivocally love and adore all kinds of pets, and we regularly visit the pet store at the new mall where cats are often for sale.

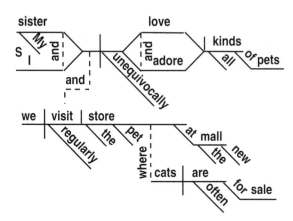

Here's another example of sentences made complicated by the addition of clauses and phrases. Breaking sentences into their components helps when faced with determining their construction.

She is the saleswoman from whom I bought my birthstone ring, the aquamarine, but I didn't buy a pair of earrings from her, or the pearl necklace that I had wanted to give to my mother as a Christmas present.

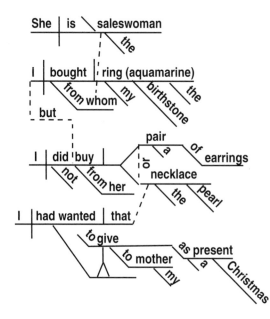

Notice how dependent clauses are anchored to independent clauses, and rely on conjunctions to make their meanings clear through the connection of one thought to another.

Activities

A. Complete the following by filling in the blanks.

Example:

A dotted line in a diagram shows the relationship or connection of one clause to another.

1. _____clauses stand alone because they are complete thoughts or sentences.

2. Gerunds, infinitives, and participles are_____.

3. A _____ lacks a subject or predicate, or both.

4. _____clauses can't stand alone because they lack a subject or verb.

5. This clause, "As soon as the teacher began lecturing, the dismissal bell rang," is a(an) _____ clause.

6. The three types of dependent clauses are: _____, _____, _____.

7. _____usually have the word *to* attached to them, and they may function as nouns, _____ , and _____.

8. Gerunds function as _____.

9. Both _____ and _____ end in the _____ suffix, but only _____ act as adjectives.

10. _____clauses may be introduced by relative adverbs or subordinating conjunctions.

11. Relative pronouns and relative adverbs introduce _____ clauses.

12. Relative adverbs serve as connectors or _____.

13. _____ clauses may function in a sentence as S, DO, OP, PN, or IO.

14. _____ use either this structure ⌐ or this one ＼___ .

15. _____ phrases contain the preposition, modifiers, and its object.

16. Subordinating conjunctions connect the adverb clause to its _____ clause.

61

B. Diagram these sentences.

Example:

Write your letter "To Whom It May Concern."

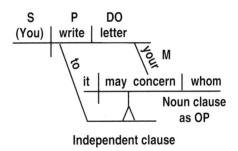

1. The boy is not sorry for what he said, even though he apologized to the girl.

2. Jake's aunt and uncle own and operate a mom-and-pop store in Salem, which they've done for years, but now they're going to sell it, even though Jake thinks that they'll greatly miss it.

3. Jimmy Carter, who was President of the United States, was a peanut farmer.

4. She left her jogging shoes at home.

5. The house I mortgage will have to fit all my needs.

6. Although it was quite early in the morning, my doorbell rang.

7. The dining room set is beautiful, but I can't afford it.

8. My mother and father live in Minneapolis because they like cool weather, but my brother moved to Chicago to be with his girlfriend, although I think that they've recently broken up over differences in career direction and child rearing.

9. Royce likes to go wherever there's action.

10. Having given it much thought, I decided, in the end, to stay and not worry about it.

11. The account executive whom we just hired brought in three new clients.

12. The book which I authored related my UFO experiences.

13. What you did is inexcusable, and you, who should know better, ought to be ashamed.

1. The three main types of verbals are gerunds, infinitives, and participles.

2. Adverb clauses rely on independent structures to complete their meaning; they modify verbs, adjectives, and adverbs, and are introduced by subordinating conjunctions.

3. Adjective clauses are dependent structures modifying nouns and pronouns, and are introduced by relative pronouns and relative adverbs.

4. Noun clauses are dependent structures that function as Ss, DOs, OPs, PNs, IOs, APs; noun clauses don't modify any part of speech.

5. A compound sentence has two or more independent clauses; a complex sentence has at least one independent clause connected to at least one dependent clause; and a **compound-complex** sentence has at least two independent clauses as well as at least one dependent clause.

Phrase and Clause Box

	Structure	Special Trait	Function	Modify	Example	Diagramming Note
1.	gerund	ends in "ing"	as Noun: S, PN, DO, OP, AP		Jogging is good	Gerund
2.	infinitive	usually has "to"	as Noun: S, DO, PN, AP Adj Adv	nouns and pronouns verbs, adjectives, or other adverbs	He wanted to be first.	Infinitive
3.	participle	ends in "ing" or "ed," "n," "e," "en"	as Adj:	nouns and pronouns	Bob had a swimming party.	Participle
4.	adjective clause	connected by relative pronouns, and relative adverbs	as Adj:	nouns and pronouns	I like swimming, but I can't stand the heat.	
5.	noun clause	relative pronouns or other connectives	as Nouns: S, DO OP, PN, IO, AP		What she did upset me.	
6.	adverb clause	begin with SCs	as Adverbs	verbs adverbs adjectives	I'll call if you want.	
7.	prep. phrase	P, its O, M	as Adj or Adv	nouns, verbs, adj, adv, prns.	She visited after the game.	Preposition
8.	appositive	explains, renames or identifies word	as a restrictive or non-restrictive phrase or clause		Mary, my friend, lives nearby.	

-

Using the legend in the front of the book, diagram all of the following sentences.

Example:

The baby cried with zeal.

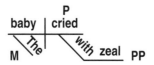

1. Will Bobby sing?

2. Register here.

3. Cameron looked worried.

4. He hates spinach.

5. The Bradfords bought a motorhome.

6. Paige is on time.

7. Vince ran to the store.

8. Cross the street carefully.

9. The little boy laughed over the video on kittens.

10. Lynne, Amanda, and I went to the movies.

11. Either Carter or Joe will be my teammate.

12. Vicki and Kim rented a video and watched it until late last night.

13. My English professor and I wrote, directed, and produced our college's musical of Broadway songs.

14. Kasey, Steve, Cary, Byron, Scarlett, and Jana play a variety of instruments and have formed a combo.

15. None of the gang went to the theater or rented a movie at Blockbuster video store.

16. Don't judge him or her.

17. Will you or Barry call your parents or write home?

18. Rosie and Paul got married and went on a long honeymoon to the Adirondacks.

19. Is he tall, dark, and handsome?

20. A girl wore wire-rim glasses, a short skirt, and spiked heels.

21. Two thousand or three thousand boys and girls jammed the orange and green stadium in anticipation of the rock group's appearance.

22. Shy and scared Caroline easily and correctly answered the questions on the oral and written exams for her doctoral degree.

23. Disadvantaged and under-privileged cultural minorities are applying for state and federal grants.

24. At the sound of the fire alarm, Cody and Yin grabbed their pants and ran outside, across the street for quick and reassuring help from neighbors.

25. Claudia and Trish answered the questionnaire honestly and carefully.

26. Annette wore navy blue and periwinkle shorts with white stripes, and a yellow top with a pattern of tiny flowers.

27. The city and county street workers tirelessly and diligently fixed old and decadent sewer covers, and damaged and chipped hydrants on Sixth Street.

28. Hand and canister vacuum cleaners, window and free-standing fans, and Johnson and York air conditioners are on sale until the first of the month.

29. Boisterous, loud-mouthed, and crude Adrian is actively and obviously seeking the office of class president.

30. Dan, Mark, and Becky impatiently and nervously stood on the porch and endlessly rang the doorbell.

31. Dell and I washed and waxed the royal blue Toyota with yellow and blue racing stripes, and the dark green Porsche with the white sunroof.

32. Tell Jill and Marnie about the books, the coupons, and the business cards.

33. Send me the address and phone number for your new residence.

34. Nedra and Frank eagerly and excitedly picked Hillary the leader of our small but close group of writers and artists.

35. Can you and your colleagues reduce the pain and stress of my hectic and busy life?

36. Kenny, Erin, and Professor Collins nominated and voted Bobby and Willy president and vice president respectively.

37. Little Mickey Johnson drew and colored a horse and buggy black and white.

38. Did Dad and Mom name and choose Sis or Aunt Cathy executrix or power-of-attorney of their will?

39. The high school principal and the tenth grade math teacher appointed eleventh-grader Marshall, and senior Garrett, school representatives and student government delegates.

40. The county police and the county council often think Old Man Forester, the first council president, insane.

41. Ramon, Manuel, and Diego picked out and gave Sherry, Louella, and Lillian, roses, candy, and cards.

42. The prosecuting attorney, the arresting officer, and the store owner labeled the heavy-set and loud man, the little guy, and the tall woman thieves and felonious criminals.

43. The President of the United States read and vetoed one bill on wetlands, but she eagerly and hurriedly passed another bill on land reclamation.

44. My cousin Reggie fervently sang the first song, and I played the violin for her.

45. Today the mail was light, but tomorrow my mail box will be filled with envelopes, advertisements, and bills.

46. My Aunt Georgio lives in Niagara Falls, but she works on the Canadian side.

47. Exhausted and sleepy, Marty sluggishly and aimlessly rose from the bed and showered before breakfast, and then he left for work on time.

48. Either Earnest or Brock is going, but I don't know when.

49. Cousin Lyle and his wife, Maya, live and work in Seattle, but they're from Erie originally.

50. Gus bought a pair of red neon and orange-striped shorts, and a fancy, tailored shirt, but his brother didn't get anything.

51. I applied to UCLA, but Yale accepted me first.

52. "Crazy" Ed admitted to the crime, but "Snake" was the perpetrator.

53. Are you going to guarantee the motherboard in the computer and fix the stuck key on the keyboard, or will you send me an entirely new and warranted computer which should be given to me because of the aggravation I have had with this computer system?

54. Roxane has to deliver the newspaper before six in the morning.

55. To forgive wholeheartedly is to love unconditionally.

56. The gusting wind feels too powerful to walk in.

57. Madge introduced the Honorable Andrew Brady, city mayor, after Father Luke Donati gave the blessing.

58. Jumping rope and jogging are good exercises for strengthening muscles, but you must be careful not to overdo, as damage to tendons could result, unless you do warm-ups and cool-downs.

59. Although John took private and expensive driving lessons, he still flunked the driving part of the exam which many teenagers seem to fail on the first try.

60. The minister knows that you're the cantor for next Sunday's morning sermon.

61. The novel that you finished was written by Sinclair Lewis.

62. There's a lot to do at the new amusement park, but make sure to bring enough money unless you expect to win a bundle.

63. Honey, before you speak, think first because a wrong word uttered could upset the CEO who isn't a patient and understanding woman.

64. Gosh, sweetheart! The sunset is absolutely beautiful when the sky has a pink tinge to it.

65. My son, who's a civil engineer for the city, wants to return to school for his master's degree, and then he plans on opening his own business.

66. In researching the job market, Bentley learned that he had to better prepare by getting a college degree and relevant training.

67. No, I don't want to hear about discovering a new way to get the job done.

68. Look out! A train's coming, and we're sitting on the tracks, and you haven't started the car's engine.

69. Wait! Don't go without me unless you're going to conduct the seminar by yourself and without the help of an expert like me.

70. The building contractor, who is our old and valued friend, is going to build an 18 X 20 addition for us, but he said the roofer would put in a skylight or two.

71. Heavens! Traveling by car from Maryland to Oregon is long, boring, and exhausting; but I began reading a book whenever I wasn't driving, so time passed quickly, although by having lost the directions, we were late arriving at our destination.

72. Yea! There's nothing to do today, which means I can leave early to do errands and buy a fancy, gold and silver bracelet for my birthday, which costs more than I want to pay.

73. If you'll show me the way to Queens, I'll be able to make my singing classes on time, providing that your directions are clear and accurate.

74. The play that I didn't like had a futuristic plot to it.

75. Would you like to visit Uncle Chris in New Orleans, or would you prefer to stay home and study for your final exams?

Answers

Diagnostic Exam, Page iv.

1. Push the button.

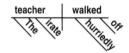

2. The irate teacher hurriedly walked off.

3. Bob and Mary are working.

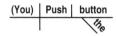

4. Mary cooks and serves.

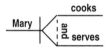

5. Brandi was cooking and baking.

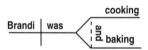

6. José and Rosella work and play.

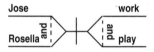

7. When will you leave?

8. They were jailed without counsel or a phone call.

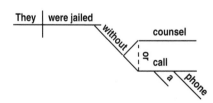

9. They sang very loudly in their high school chorus.

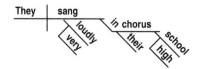

10. Here comes the team.

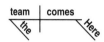

11. His gray cat is a skinny Siamese.

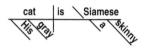

12. Kendra attended a cook's conference.

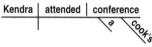

13. Her mother gave her a birthday present.

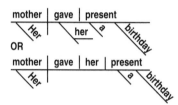

14. Over the hills and through the woods traveled our sled.

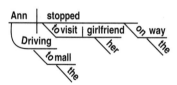

15. Driving to the mall, Ann stopped on the way to visit her girlfriend.

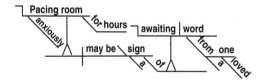

16. Pacing a room anxiously for hours may be a sign of awaiting word from a loved one.

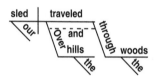

17. Courtney is working on the computer.

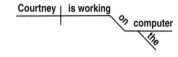

18. Mark is studying to pass the SATs.

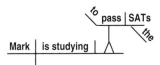

19. Vote for Sam for class president.

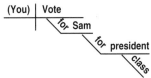

20. Our French class and the teacher are taking a trip to beautiful Paris.

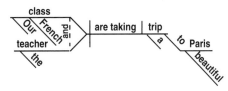

21. The best food in any restaurant often can be found in family diners.

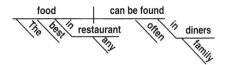

22. Sarah sat and wrote her first book.

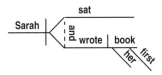

23. The teacher read the short story, and then he explained the plot.

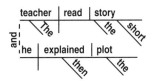

24. The computer you bought is a clone.

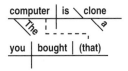

25. This is the house that Jack built.

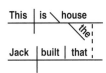

Chapter One, Page 4.

A.

1. Nancy Kerrigan won the Silver Medal for skating in the 1994 Winter Olympics.

2. My Aunt Dolores makes the best pasta.

3. Sister Marilyn taught college English in 1985.

4. The thick, blinding snow paralyzed the city of Erie.

5. Isn't Ocean City, Maryland, a top, East Coast resort?

6. Margaret Garner wanted to kill her child to spare her from having to return to slavery.

7. John Austin prefers studying literature over biology.

8. Holly plans on attending art school after graduating from high school.

9. All weekend long, Brynne Alysen worked on her science project.

10. (You) Please knock before entering.

B.

1. imperative; complex; period
2. declarative; simple; period
3. exclamatory; simple; exclamation point
4. interrogative; complex; question mark
5. exclamatory or imperative; simple; exclamation point
6. declarative; simple; period
7. declarative; simple; period
8. interrogative; compound; question mark
9. exclamatory; simple; two exclamation points
10. declarative; simple; period

C.

    <ins>   S   </ins>   <ins>   P   </ins>
  M N   V   PP
1. The osprey soared into the clouds.

       <ins>   S   </ins>   <ins>   P   </ins>
  M M N   V   M   M   M   N
2. The old man saluted the United States flag
<ins>SC   S   PP</ins>
as the parade for the Vietnam soldiers
  V   M
marched past.

   <ins> S </ins>   <ins>   P   </ins>
  N   V   M   PP   PP
3. Heather walked slowly to the far corner of the
room.

    <ins>   S   </ins>   <ins>   P   </ins>
  M   N   V M N M M
4. The pediatrician gave the child a rubella
    N
vaccination.

    <ins>   S   </ins>   <ins>   P   </ins>
  M   N   V M N   PP
5. The secretary used a computer for the report.

    <ins>   S   </ins>   <ins>   P   </ins>
  M   N   V M M N   PP
6. The dentist filled a large cavity in my back
tooth.

  <ins> S </ins>   <ins>   P   </ins>
  N   V M N
7. Bobby needed a passport.

   <ins> S </ins>   <ins>   P   </ins>
  N   V M M   N   PP
8. Derrick wanted a counselor's job at the
summer camp.

   <ins> S </ins>   <ins>   P   </ins>
  N   V M N   PP   PP
9. Jerry wrote a letter of complaint to the
company president.

     <ins>   P   </ins>
    V M N
10. Pump the brakes.

  <ins> P </ins> <ins> S </ins>   <ins> P </ins>
  V Prn V Prn M N
11. Will you tell me the truth?

 <ins> S </ins>   <ins>   P   </ins>
Prn V M N   PP   Prn V M
12. He's a waterman in Maryland who works the
      N   N
Chesapeake Bay.

D.

1. F; no punctuation   5. Frag; no S
2. C; has S and P   6. Frag; no P
3. Frag; no P   7. F; no punctuation
4. C; has S and P   8. C; has S and P

E. Answers will vary

Chapter Two, Page 10.

A.

    P DO S
1. Play ball. (You)

    M   S   P M DO
2. My brother built a cabaña.

     S   P   M   DO   PP
3. She bought the typewriter at a garage sale.

     S   P   IO M DO
4. She offered me her C.D.

       P   IO M DO   S
5. Hand Terry the beans. (You)

       P M P IO M   DO   S
6. Don't ask me any questions. (You)

       S   C   S   P   PP
7. Sarah and Derrick were on the same team.

     M   M   S   P PA
8. The television picture is blurry.

    S P   M DO   PP
9. I visited my mother in Pittsburgh.

      S   PM M M PN
10. Today's not a good day.

B.

1. S (or N) + P (or V); intransitive
2. S + P + DO; transitive
3. S + P(LV) + PA; intransitive
4. S + P + DO; transitive
5. S + P + IO + DO; transitive
6. S + P + DO + OC(N); transitive
7. S + P + DO + OC(Adj); transitive
8. S + P + DO + OC(Adj); transitive
9. S + P (LV) + PA; intransitive

10. S + P + DO + OC(Adj); transitive

11. S + P (LV) + PN; intransitive

12. S + P + DO + OC(N); transitive

C.

                             S   P   DO
1. The animal rescue worker climbed the tree
          PP
  after the dog.

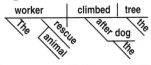

      S   P   DO   PP
2. (You) Draw a big picture of a pony.

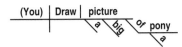

          S   P OC(Adj)
3. The skater is exhausted.

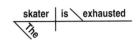

        S   S   S   P   DO
4. Craig, George, and Kevin batted the ball
  around.

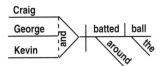

   S   P   DO   P   DO   P DO
5. Allyce writes books, gives speeches, and sells Avon.

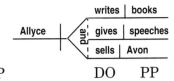

    S   P   DO   PP
6. You spent too much time on this book.

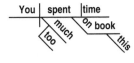

        S   PP   P   DO
7. The woman with two grown children plays piano.

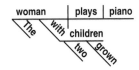

         S   P IO OC(Adj)
8. Doctors always make me nervous.

                S   P   DO
9. Troy drives a fancy, red Mustang.

       S   P   OC(Adj)   PP
10. Kim looked pretty in her new dress.

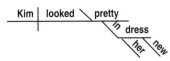

  S   S   P   (LV) IO   DO
11. Wendy and Joy won't tell him the answer.

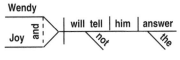

      S   P   IO   DO
12. I offered Alexis the sales job.

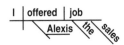

D.

        S(N)   P(V)   IO(N)   DO(N)
1. Whitney gave Shelly her book.

          S(N) P(V)   OC(Adj)
2. The soup was excellent.

      S(N)   S(N)   P(V)   OC(Adj)
3. Bobby and Tommy seem upset over their
  accident.

     S(Prn) P(V)   DO(N)
4. I   want a new car for my birthday.

      S(N)   S(N)   S(N)   P(V)
5. Polly, Amanda, and Brandon arrived on time.

     S(Prn) P(V)   IO(N)   DO(N)
6. I   made Roxie a cheese pizza.

      S(N)   S(Prn) P(V)   IO(N)   DO(N)
7. Daddy and I bought you baseball cards for your
  collection.

   S(Prn) P(V)   IO(N)   IO(N)   DO(N)
8. I   gave Spencer and Travis a new camera for
  their birthdays.

     S(Prn) P(LV)   DO(N)   OC(N)
9. We shall call Kitty Ebony.

     S(Prn) P(V)   IO(N)   DO(N)
10. (You) Give Sr. Leone our love.

Review Test 1, Page 13.

I.

  1. C; has S (You) and P

  2. C; has S and P

  3. R; needs punctuation

4. R; needs comma before "especially"

5. R; needs punctuation

6. F; no P

7. C; has S (You) and P

8. F; no P

9. C; has S and P

10. C; has S and P

II.

1. The little girl behind me cried at the loss of her dog.

girl | cried   S + P

2. The irate patron suddenly walked off.

patron | walked   S + P

3. Carl and Brian play baseball and jog.

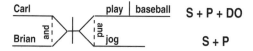

Carl / Brian (and) — play | baseball   S + P + DO
— jog   S + P

4. Where have you been?

you | have been   S + P(LV)

5. Barbara sang quite well.

Barbara | sang   S + P

6. The parasailor soared quickly, and silently flew away.

parasailor | soared / (and) flew   S + P + P

7. Our cock-a-poo is black.

cock-a-poo | is \ black   S + P + PA

8. Don't eat so fast.

(You) | Do eat   S + P(LV)

9. Kelsey's softball team practices every day.

team | practices   S + P

10. Are you the band director?

you | Are \ director   S + P + PN

11. Well! I never!

Not a Sentence.

12. Fire!

Not a Sentence.

13. She looks pretty in white.

She | looks \ pretty   S + P + OC(Adj)

14. The freshman class elected Bart leader.

class | elected | Bart \ leader   S + P + IO + OC(N)

15. The waves ripped through the resort area.

waves | ripped   S + P

16. Give the hummingbird nectar.

(You) | Give | hummingbird | nectar   S + P + IO + DO

17. John Wayne's real name was Marion Morrison.

name | was \ Marion Morrison   S + P + PN

18. Count your blessings.

(You) | Count | blessings   S + P + DO

19. Master Maid, Country Caterers, and Mr. Clean cook and clean.

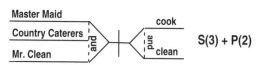

Master Maid / Country Caterers / Mr. Clean (and) — cook / (and) clean   S(3) + P(2)

20. Sam and Greg are playing hockey.

Sam / Greg (and) — are playing | hockey   S + P(LV) + DO

III.

Sentence		
S	P	C
1. NPR	broadcasts	programs = DO
2. Regia	experiences	attacks = DO
3. Leslie	wants	to be actress = Inf/DO
4. Clichés	erode	writing = DO
5. Senate	declared	law = DO
		unconstitutional = OC(Adj)
6. (You)	Do find	defendant = DO
		guilty = OC(Adj)
7. Kara	is	neighbor = PN
		babysitter = PN
8. Jessica	considers	herself = DO;
		lucky = OC(Adj)
9. girls	think	team = DO; best = OC(Adj)
10. teacher	determined	suggestions = DO
		costly = OC(Adj)
11. I	thought	myself = DO; shy = OC(Adj)

12. party   was   success = PN
he   gave   it = DO
13. Marty,   are   nurses = PN
Harry
14. (You)   See   flower = DO
15. person   handed   Margaret = IO
packages = DO
16. (You)   Bring   stack = DO

IV.

    M   P   IO   M   DO   PP
1. Please make me address labels on your
                      S
computer. (You)
    P M S   P   M   DO   PP
2. Didn't you staple those papers in that pile?
    S   P   P   M DO   PP
3. Ken's buying a house on the water.
       S   P   P   PP   PP
4. Everyone's worrying about the pollution in
Puget Sound.
       P   M   C P   M   S
5. Spring forward, and fall back. (You)
     M   M   S   P   M   M
6. Some T.V. networks offer only mindless
       DO
programs.
     S   P PN   PP   PP
7. New York City is one of the best cities for
national and international businesses.
     M   S   P   PP   PP
8. My family went on a trip through the New
England area.
     M   M   M   S   P   C
9. Saint John's junior class produced and
       P   DO
presented *My Fair Lady*.
     S   C   S   P   P   DO
10. Sam and Greg are playing hockey.
     P DO   S
11. Help me! (You)
       S   P   PP
12. Perry Como comes from Canonsburg.
     S P   M M DO C M S   P   P
13. I bought the red roses but the vase was given
     PP
to me.
       S   C   S   P   M DO   PP
14. Maxine and Rolanda escaped the fire without
getting burned.

         Gerund   N(DO)   P   M
15. Diagramming sentences requires critical
   DO
thinking.

V.

Sentence

	Function	Structure	Puntuation
1.	interrogative	S	? question mark
2.	declarative	S	. period
3.	imperative	S	. period
4.	exclamatory	S	! exlamation point
5.	interrogative	S	? question mark
6.	imperative	S	! exclamation point
7.	declarative	Compound	. period
8.	declarative	Complex	. period
9.	declarative	Compound	. period
10.	declarative	S	. period
11.	imperative	S	. period
12.	declarative	S	. period
13.	interrogative	S	? question mark
14.	declarative	S	. period
15.	declarative	S	. period
16.	declarative	S	. period
17.	declarative	S	. period
18.	declarative	S	. period
19.	declarative	Compound	. period
20.	declarative	S	. period

Chapter Three, Page 21.

A. N-once, PN-twice, cont-3.

1. My mother has macular degeneration, an eye disorder.

2. Kenny got a counselor's job at my brother's summer camp.

3. It's up to you.

4. Her garden needs weeding.

5. Horton's Pharmacy has your prescription filled.

6. Tracy and Vince themselves designed their own wedding.

7. Have you practiced your lines for the play?

8. Will somebody answer me—whoever is there?

9. The president offered Nancy and me a job with the company.

10. Mine are heavier and larger.

B.

1. she
2. he
3. It's
4. me
5. us
6. them
7. her
8. they
9. themselves
10. himself

C.

1. subject
2. subject
3. subject
4. subject
5. subject
6. subject
7. object
8. object
9. object
10. object

D.

1. This is the right way.

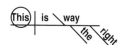

2. Who's the lady with Peter?

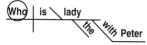

3. That is an Air Force plane.

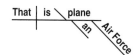

4. She and I work hard and play tirelessly.

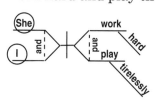

5. The pie came from my neighbor.

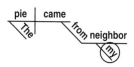

6. All of us took English 101.

7. Who's reading the book?

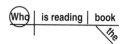

8. Sleep soundly.

9. He or she will give us the album.

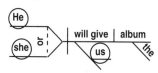

10. We come from New York City.

Chapter Four, Page 26.

A.

	Voice	Mood	Mode	Tense	Person
1.	active	indicative	fact	past	3rd-sing.
2.	active	imperative	necessity	present	2nd- s or plu.
3.	passive	interr.	fact	past prog	3rd-s
4.	passive	indicative	fact	future	1st-s
5.	passive	subjunctive	ability	past	1st-s
6.	active	indicative	fact	past	3rd-p
7.	active	imperative	necessity	present	2nd-s or p
8.	active	indicative	fact	past	3rd-p
9.	passive	indicative	ability	fut.-perf	3rd-s
10.	passive	indicative	ability	present	3rd-s
11.	passive	indicative	ability	fut.-prog	3rd-s
12.	passive	indicative	fact	pres-prog	1st-s

B.

                                         DO
1. Travis and Brianna <u>baptized</u> their first child
  OC(N)
  Carrie Marie.

                   IO   DO
2. Grandma <u>made</u> me Toll House cookies.

        IO   DO
3. <u>Pass</u> me the ketchup please.

                         DO
4. My brother <u>figures</u> math problems on his
    computer.

                DO   OC(Adj)
5. The teen <u>painted</u> his Prelude a neon red.

              DO   OC(N)
6. We <u>nominated</u> Bubba "Most Valuable Player."

7. Chandler, Tom, and Cheynie <u>painted</u> their club
  DO   OC(Adj)
  house gingerbread brown.

           DO OC(Adj)
8. <u>Do</u> you <u>think</u> me pretty?

                DO   OC(N)
9. We never <u>thought</u> her a good teacher.

                       DO
10. Dr. Stockard <u>considered</u> her college class
  OC(Adj) OC(Adj)
    rude and loud.

                     DO OC(Adj)
11. My Uncle Harry <u>bought</u> the stereo cheap.

              DO   DO
12. Rover and Fido <u>did</u> tricks and <u>jumped</u> hoops.

          DO OC(Adj) OC(Adj)
13. She <u>called</u> him lazy and spoiled.

             DO OC(Adj)
14. Maxine <u>thought</u> the song melodious.

       DO OC(N)
15. <u>Consider</u> her a failure.

                IO   DO
16. The mail carrier <u>gave</u> her a letter.

                  DO
17. <u>Did</u> you <u>play</u> that tune on the piano or on the
    organ?

C.

1. Julio painted the flag red, white, and blue.

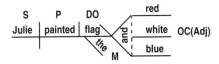

2. The tale about the raven made me scared.

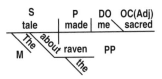

3. Will you shut the door?

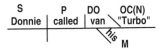

4. Donnie called his van "Turbo."

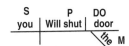

5. Bessie thinks her condo beautiful.

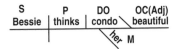

6. The club thought the speaker excellent.

7. Brynne's referee called her safe.

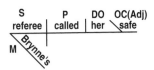

8. Marlo imagined the book's murderer tall,
heavy, and bearded.

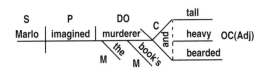

9. The Three Musketeers handed me their
swords.

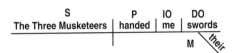

10. Ask your teacher those questions.

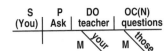

11. Send me a copy.

12. Gramps built Zeb a tackle box.

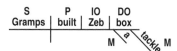

13. Mrs. Black sold you a fax machine.

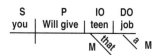

14. Will you give that teen a job?

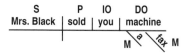

15. Don't give him any answers.

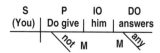

16. Will you send her flowers?

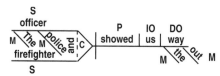

17. The police officer and firefighter showed us the way out.

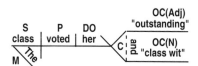

18. The class voted her "outstanding" and "class wit."

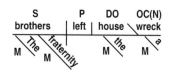

19. The fraternity brothers left the house a wreck.

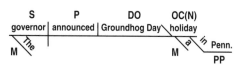

20. The governor announced Groundhog Day a holiday in Pennsylvania.

D. Answers will vary.

Review Test 2, Page 29.

I.

      PRP
1. Emily Dickinson was a great poet.

   PRP
2. Martin found his wallet in his pants pocket.

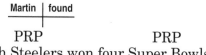

           PRP   PRP
3. The Pittsburgh Steelers won four Super Bowls.

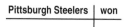

        PRP
4. The Caribbean Sea is filled with jewels of underwater life.

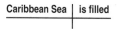

 PRP   PRP
5. Meg and I are Lambda Chi Rho sorority sisters
                     PRP
who live at the Riverside sorority house.

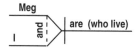

6. We'll get you a new clock radio since your brother broke your last one.

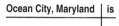

           PRP
7. Ocean City, Maryland, is a family resort on the coast.

8. The manta ray is a large animal living in tropical waters.

9. A Hovercraft is a vehicle that travels in air, over water, and on smooth ground surfaces.

10. A system of reading for the blind is called
   PRP
Braille.

          PRP   PRP

11. The author, Edgar Allan Poe, died in Baltimore;

his works are often bizarre and eerie.

```
author | died

works  | are
```

          PRP   PRP

12. Broadway is the theater district of New York
City.

```
Broadway | is
```

           PRP   PRP

13. Ho Chi Minh City is the capital of South

                             PRP

Vietnam; it used to be called Saigon.

```
Ho Chi Minh City | is  (it used)        S   P
                                        it | used
```

14. Go! (You)

```
(You) | Go
```

                   PRP

15. Will you watch little Gregory for me tonight?

```
you | Will watch
```

II.

1. medium = media   9. parenthesis = parentheses
2. churches = church   10. foci = focus
3. criteria = criterion   11. teeth = tooth
4. penny = pennies   12. datum = data
5. hooves = hoof   13. curricula = curriculum
6. geese = goose   14. cherub = cherubim
7. deer = deer   15. knives = knife
8. crises = crisis   16. fungus = fungi

III.

1. girls dresses = girls'('s)   6. razors = razors'('s)
2. child playroom = child's   7. quarters = quarter's(s')
3. dogs bone = dogs'('s)   8. man = man's
4. fox den = fox's   9. author = author's
5. knifes handle = knife's   10. kids = kid's(s')

IV.

       PRP   N

1. *Little Women* is a movie classic.

```
      S          P    PN
"Little Women" | is \ classic
```

     PRP   N

2. Tom Clancy wrote the best-selling novel,

     PRP

The Hunt for Red October.

```
    S          P      DO          APP
Tom Clancy | wrote | novel (Red October)
```

   PRP   N   Prn N

3. Barry didn't offer a pregnant woman his seat

        N

on the bus.

```
  S       P        DO
Barry | did offer | seat
       \ not    \ woman
                   IO
```

        N   PRP   N

4. The guitar teacher gave Mary Ellen lessons on

     PRP

Thursdays.

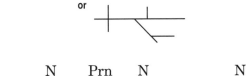

         N   Prn N   N

5. The trees in her backyard were dogwoods and

   N

cherries.

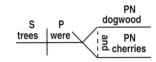

       PRP   N

6. Barbara Stanwyck was a famous actress.

```
       S            P     PN
Barbara Stanwyck | was \ actress
```

 Prn   Prn

7. You and he were funny.

```
     S
    You
    S   and   P     PA
    he      were \ funny
```

  Prn

8. Mine are better.

```
  S     P     PA
Mine | are \ better
```

78

Prn
9. Didn't you finish?

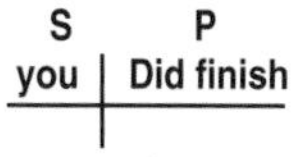
S
P
you
Did finish

Prn N
10. This isn't the catalogue here.

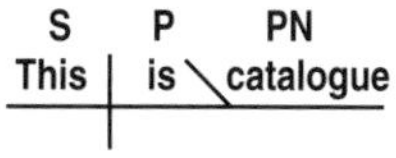
S
P
PN
This
is
catalogue

Prn
11. Everyone was friendly.

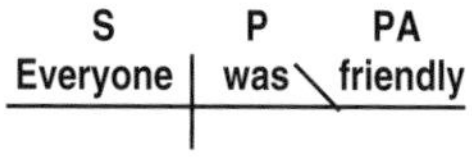
S
P
PA
Everyone
was
friendly

12. No one has been around here.

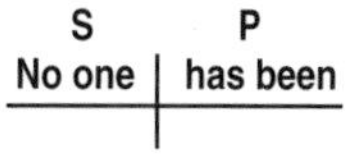
S
P
No one
has been

Prn N
13. All of the flowers are blossoming.

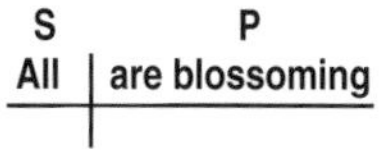
S
P
All
are blossoming

N
14. The writers' organization considered the
N N-Ger
presenter on book publishing excellent.

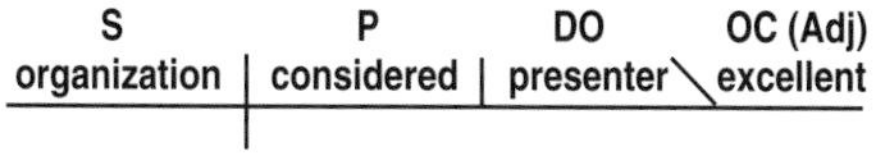
S
P
DO
OC (Adj)
organization
considered
presenter
excellent

Prn
15. Don't you care?

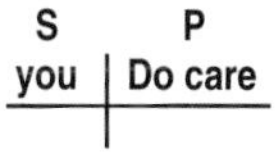
S
P
you
Do care

V.

S C S P DO M C P
1. Clowns and mimes did tricks well and gave
IO DO
people laughter.

S P DO M OC(N)
2. (You) Consider it a success.

S P M DO M OC(Adj)
3. Barnes considered his class quite smart and
M OC(Adj)
very creative.

S M P M DO M M
4. She reluctantly painted her room a deep
OC(Adj)
orchid.

S S C S P M P
5. Meg, Bobby, and Larry did not (didn't) make
M DO C M DO OC(Adj)
their teachers and their principal happy.

Sentences

Voice	Mood	Mode	Tense	Person
1. passive	ind	interrog.	future	2nd-s, p
2. passive	ind	ability	present	3rd-s
3. active	ind	concl.	past/pres./pres.	2nd1st-s; 3rd-s
4. active	ind	courage	past	3rd-s
5. active	imp	necessity	present	2nd-s
6. passive	ind	ability	pres./pres.	2nd-s, p; 1st-s
7. passive	ind	intent	future prog	3rd-s
8. active	imp	fact	present	2nd-s, p
9. passive	subj	permission	present	2nd-s, p; 1st-s
10. passive	ind	fact	present	3rd-s

Chapter Five, Page 38.

A.

1. Fighting is no way to settle a disagreement.
2. He was proud to have been selected for the National Guard.
3. To live happily ever after is everyone's dream.
4. Learning to drive for the first time is frightening.
5. Rebecca fears walking alone at night in the big city.
6. Lenny hates driving in rush hour traffic.
7. All night, Mariette heard her neighbor playing the sax.
8. The plane, buffeted by severe air currents, bounced around enough to cause air sickness in some passengers.
9. Chained to a stake, the Doberman barked for hours.
10. Approaching the street vendor, Helen bought a chili dog.

11. (Telling) the difference between identical twins isn't easy.

12. Wasn't she going to see her again?

B.

1. To be a best-selling author takes talent and experience.

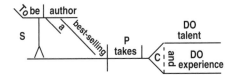

2. To err is human, and to forgive is divine.

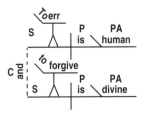

3. Losing her wallet sent Jill into a spin.

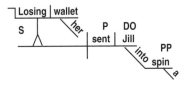

4. Dugan's preoccupied with selling crafts.

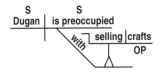

5. Thinking about the accident upset her.

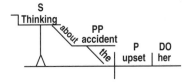

6. Following her mom's example, she's studying to be a doctor.

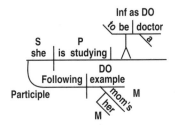

7. To study for my literature exam, I need to borrow your book.

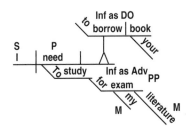

8. The supervisor is the one to see about the job.

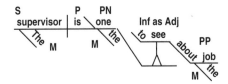

9. Marie's too sick to go.

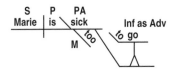

10. The music playing around us is too loud for us.

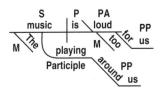

11. Hiking and picking flora are not my "thing."

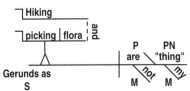

12. My brother is always looking for ways to sell used cars.

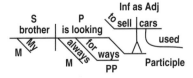

13. The farmer hates to go to the city to sell his products.

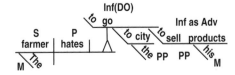

14. Blowing out cake candles, the toddler clapped and jumped.

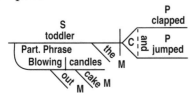

15. Making a mistake is perfectly natural and human.

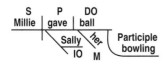

16. Millie gave Sally her bowling ball.

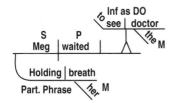

17. Holding her breath, Meg waited to see the doctor.

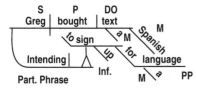

18. Intending to sign up for a language, Greg bought a Spanish text.

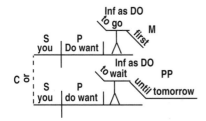

19. Do you want to go first, or do you want to wait until tomorrow?

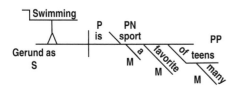

20. Swimming is a favorite sport of many teens.

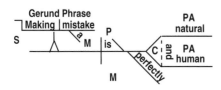

21. Painting pine cones is a fun Christmas craft.

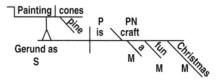

22. Boating on the lake was exciting.

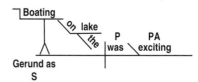

C.
1. trans: covered, intrans: hid
2. intrans: will hurry
3. trans: is reading
4. intrans: became
5. intrans: does live
6. trans: gave
7. intrans: is
8. intrans: smells
9. trans: remind
10. trans: made
11. trans: list
12. trans: put
13. intrans: is
14. intrans: are
15. trans: did see

Chapter Six, Page 44.
A.
1. green
2. brightly
3. tightly
4. C
5. C
6. C
7. happier
8. C
9. C
10. fat
11. fatter
12. C

B.
1. F
2. F
3. T
4. T
5. T
6. F
7. F
8. F
9. F

C.

1. As long as I'm in charge, changes will be made.　　adv

2. You must go before the teacher arrives.　　adv

3. Uncle Bob, who is my mother's brother, will visit tomorrow.　　adj

4. The motorist who stopped to change our tire is a relative.　　adj

5. I'll dial the number if you'll talk to her.　　adv

6. The movie [that] he scripted will be on television next year.　　adj

7. The little girl who had come to our door was selling Girl Scout cookies.　　adj

8. Give the teacher some reason why you missed her class.　　adj

9. Hollan didn't go to church because he had the flu.　　adv

10. I'll read the directions after I remove all the parts from the box.　　adv

D.

1. Barbara is well.　　well; PA

Barbara | is \ well

2. He dances well.　　well; adv

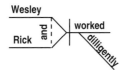

He | dances \ well

3. Everything seems blurry with my new glasses.　　blurry; PA

Everything | seems \ blurry

4. The prisoner's cell looked neat.　　neat; PA

cell | looked \ neat

5. The no-bake, chocolate cookies were absolutely magnificent.　　magnificent; PA

cookies | were \ magnificent

6. Wesley and Rick diligently worked on their lab report.　　diligently; adv

Wesley
and
Rick \ worked \ diligently

7. Delia and Millie are reliable baby-sitters and serious students.　　none　none

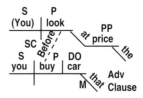

Delia
and
Millie | are | babysitters
and
students

8. It is finished.　　none

It | is finished

9. They call me Mr. Tibbs.　　none

They | call | me \ Mr. Tibbs

10. They will never go for your idea.　　never; adv

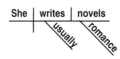

They | will go \ never

11. She loudly announced the news.　　loudly; adv

She | announced | news \ loudly

12. She usually writes romance novels.　　usually; adv
　　　　　　　　　　　　romance; adj

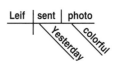

She | writes | novels \ usually \ romance

13. Never call me.　　never; adv

(You) | call | me \ Never

14. Yesterday Leif sent her a colorful photo.　　yesterday; adv
　　　　　　　　　　　　colorful; adj

Leif | sent | photo \ Yesterday \ colorful

15. Reuben quit.　　none

Reuben | quit

E.

1. Before you buy that car, look at the price.

S　P
(You) | look
SC　　　PP
S　P DO　at price
you | buy | car　the
M \ that　Adv Clause
Before

82

2. The Victorian house I always wanted was too expensive. (The word "that" is understood.)

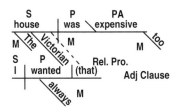

3. Mrs. Fowler is the real estate agent from whom my husband and I purchased our house.

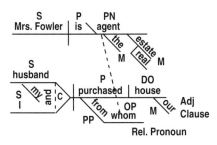

4. If you wait, I'll meet you.

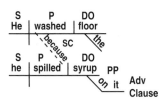

5. He washed the floor because he spilled syrup on it.

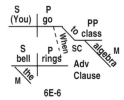

6. When the bell rings, go to algebra class.

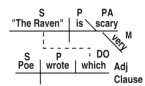

7. "The Raven," which Poe wrote, is very scary.

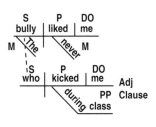

8. The bully who kicked me during recess never liked me.

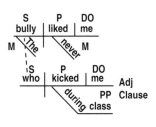

9. She's a teacher whom I had in third grade.

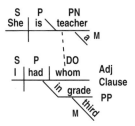

F.

	Adjectives			Adverbs	
Pos.	Comp.	Super.	Pos.	Comp.	Super.
1. good	better	best	bad	worse	worst
2. much	more	most	angrily	more angrily	most angrily
3. cold	colder	coldest	soon	sooner	soonest
4. quick	quicker	quickest	well	better	best
5. high	higher	highest	jealously	more jealously	most jealously
6. bad	worse	worst	cold	colder	coldest

Review Test 3, Page 47.

I.

1. The explosives have been activated by the demolition team.   P

2. The vase was broken by the twin brothers.   P

3. He broke out into a rash.   A

4. She designs high-tech musical equipment.   A

5. The raging "nor'easter" cancelled the festival A

6. Coordinating conjunctions link independent clauses.   A

7. Eat five vegetables and fruits a day to maintain good health.   A

8. The window panes have been washed by Karen.   P

9. Although salt adds flavor to food, it can lead to heart problems.   A

10. Do you think before you speak?   A

11. Johnson & Johnson, Proctor & Gamble, and Coca-Cola are major advertisers.   A

12. It's by far better to give than to receive.   A

13. Jogging early in the morning is safer than running in afternoon heat.   A

14. Writing lab reports frightens many students.   A

83

II.

1.
$$
\begin{array}{ll}
\quad\;\; \text{S} \qquad\qquad \text{P} \\
\text{The explosives have been activated by the} \\
\quad \text{PP} \\
\text{demolition team}
\end{array}
$$

2.
$$
\begin{array}{l}
\text{M} \quad \text{S} \quad\;\; \text{P} \qquad\;\; \text{PP} \\
\text{The vase was broken by the twin brothers.}
\end{array}
$$

3.
$$
\begin{array}{l}
\text{S} \;\; \text{P} \quad \text{M} \quad\; \text{PP} \\
\text{He broke out into a rash.}
\end{array}
$$

4.
$$
\begin{array}{l}
\text{S} \quad\; \text{P} \qquad \text{M} \qquad \text{M} \qquad \text{DO} \\
\text{She designs high-tech musical equipment.}
\end{array}
$$

5.
$$
\begin{array}{l}
\text{M} \qquad \text{M} \qquad \text{S} \qquad\quad \text{P} \qquad \text{M} \quad \text{O} \\
\text{The raging "nor'wester" cancelled the festival.}
\end{array}
$$

6.
$$
\begin{array}{ll}
\qquad\;\; \text{M} \qquad\qquad \text{S} \qquad\; \text{P} \qquad \text{M} \\
\text{Coordinating conjunctions link independent} \\
\quad \text{DO} \\
\text{clauses.}
\end{array}
$$

7.
$$
\begin{array}{ll}
\;\; \text{P} \;\; \text{M} \quad\; \text{DO} \qquad \text{C} \;\; \text{DO} \;\; \text{M} \;\; \text{M} \\
\text{Eat five vegetables and fruits a day to} \\
\quad\; \text{Inf} \qquad \text{M} \;\; \text{DO(Inf)} \;\; \text{S} \\
\text{maintain good health. (You)}
\end{array}
$$

8.
$$
\begin{array}{ll}
\;\; \text{M} \quad\;\; \text{M} \qquad \text{S} \qquad\;\; \text{P} \qquad\qquad \text{PP} \\
\text{The window panes have been washed by} \\
\quad \text{Karen.}
\end{array}
$$

9.
$$
\begin{array}{ll}
\quad\; \text{SC} \quad\;\; \text{S} \;\; \text{P} \quad \text{DO} \;\; \text{PP} \quad\; \text{S} \quad \text{P} \\
\text{Although salt adds flavor to food, it can lead to} \\
\quad \text{PP} \\
\text{heart problems.}
\end{array}
$$

10.
$$
\begin{array}{l}
\;\; \text{P} \;\; \text{S} \quad\; \text{P} \qquad\; \text{SC} \qquad \text{S} \quad\; \text{P} \\
\text{Do you think before you speak?}
\end{array}
$$

11.
$$
\begin{array}{ll}
\qquad\qquad \text{S} \qquad\qquad\qquad \text{S} \qquad\qquad \text{C} \\
\text{Johnson \& Johnson, Proctor \& Gamble, and} \\
\qquad\; \text{S} \qquad \text{P} \quad \text{M} \qquad \text{PN} \\
\text{Coca-Cola are major advertisers.}
\end{array}
$$

12.
$$
\begin{array}{l}
\text{(Expl)P} \;\; \text{PP} \qquad \text{PA} \quad\; \text{Inf} \qquad \text{C} \qquad \text{Inf} \\
\text{It's} \quad \text{by far better to give than to receive.}
\end{array}
$$

13.
$$
\begin{array}{ll}
\qquad\quad \text{Gerund as S} \qquad\qquad \text{P} \;\; \text{PA} \;\; \text{SC} \\
\text{Jogging early in the morning is safer than} \\
\qquad \text{Gerund as S of clause} \\
\text{running in afternoon heat.}
\end{array}
$$

14.
$$
\begin{array}{l}
\text{Gerund as S} \qquad\quad \text{P} \qquad \text{M} \quad \text{DO} \\
\text{Writing lab reports frightens many students.}
\end{array}
$$

III.

1. Call the 800 number for information.

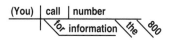

2. The wind is gusting to thirty-three mph.

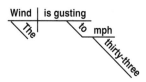

3. He broke out into a rash.

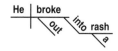

4. She designs high-tech musical equipment.

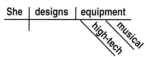

5. Eat five vegetables and fruits.

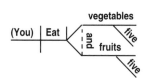

6. Just say it.

7. Do you think before you speak?

8. Johnson & Johnson, Proctor & Gamble, and Coca Cola are major advertisers.

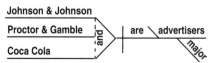

9. Greenpeace opposes any type of environmental pollution.

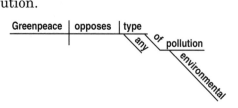

10. Did you have Mrs. Gordon for Algebra I?

```
(You) | Did have | Mrs. Gordon
                \ for Algebra I
```

11. Ariel likes to ride her bike to school.

```
           to ride | bike
                   \ to school \ her
Ariel | likes    ∧
```

IV. Fill in the chart according to degree and identify the type of modifier it is.

	Pos.	Comp.	Super.	Type
1.	high	higher	highest	(Adj)
2.	good	better	best	(Adj)
3.	little	less or lesser	least	(Adv or Adj)
4.	happily	more happily	most happily	(Adv)
5.	agreeable	more agreeable	most agreeable	(Adj)
6.	little	less	least	(Adv or Adj)
7.	happy	happier	happiest	(Adj)
8.	bravely	more bravely	most bravely	(Adv)
9.	bad	worse	worst	(Adj)
10.	soon	sooner	soonest	(Adv)
11.	good	better	best	(Adj)
12.	well	better	best	(Adv)

V. Correct the following sentences.

1. unique
2. Their, their
3. Your, than
4. through
5.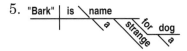
```
"Bark" | is \ name
            a \ strange \ for dog \ a
```
6. not a sentence
7.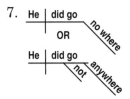
```
He | did go
         \ no where
   OR
He | did go
         \ anywhere \ not
```

Chapter Seven, Page 55.

A.

1. Observers shouldn't view solar eclipses without the aid of specially designed glasses.
2. She owns the McDonalds at Fifth and Main Streets.
3. Our dog, Cinco, smells of the outside.
4. Poems about love seem to carry a special music of their own.
5. Joanna was embarrassed by the put-down.
6. Beneath the eaves of the roof stands an old man with a cane.
7. Tell me no lies.
8. The veterans of the Vietnam War marched past the Statue of Liberty.
9. Harriet was out of her league in the State Science Competition.
10. Mrs. Ramsay, the school principal, laid down the law.

B.

1. She ate four slices of pizza and drank two glasses of Pepsi.
2. Marti still works for the Saks Fifth Avenue Company that she started with ten years ago.
3. While Donnie was playing football, he also practiced for basketball.
4. I didn't want to go because there would be too many people there.
5. He studied linguistics intensely, so he should know word derivations.
6. Whoever arrives first will have to help me with decorations.
7. Bobbette is taller than she.
8. You may talk quietly or read books.
9. Cramer was tired and exhausted.
10. He asked not only once, but also twice.

C.

1. Neither Gabe nor Becca enjoyed the dinner.

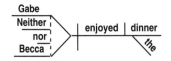
```
Gabe
Neither
  nor      enjoyed | dinner
Becca                    \ the
```

2. Well, goodness gracious, Jackie! I haven't seen you in years.

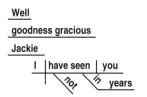

3. I bought a ticket but I really didn't want to go.

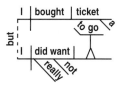

4. Breck looked around.

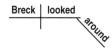

5. Jack, did you ask a question?

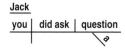

6. Hurrah! Our team won the finals.

7. Of course I did all the math.

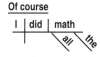

8. I put her feathered cap there.

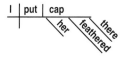

9. Help! I can't hold the box anymore.

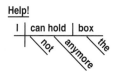

10. It was difficult to understand him.

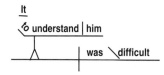

Chapter Eight, Page 61.

A.

1. Independent
2. verbals
3. fragment
4. dependent
5. adverb
6. adverb, adjective, noun
7. Infinitives, adverbs, adjectives
8. nouns
9. gerunds, participles, ing, participles
10. Adjective
11. adverb
12. conjunctions
13. Noun
14. Participles
15. Prepositional
16. Independent

B.

1. The boy is not sorry for what he said, even though he apologized to the girl.

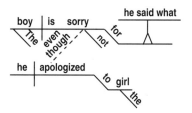

2. Jake's aunt and uncle own and operate a mom-and-pop store in Salem, which they've done for years, but now they're going to sell it, even though Jake thinks that they'll greatly miss it.

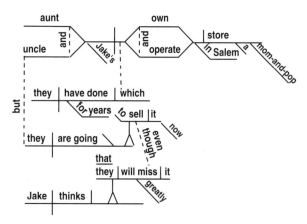

3. Jimmy Carter, who was President of the United States, was a peanut farmer.

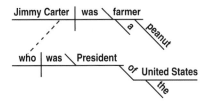

4. She left her jogging shoes at home.

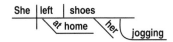

5. The house I mortgage will have to fit all my needs.

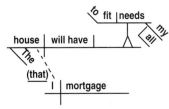

6. Although it was quite early in the morning, my doorbell rang.

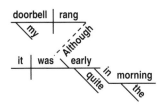

7. The dining room set is beautiful, but I can't afford it.

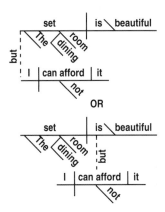

8. My mother and father live in Minneapolis because they like cool weather, but my brother moved to Chicago to be with his girlfriend, although I think that they've recently broken up over differences in career direction and child rearing.

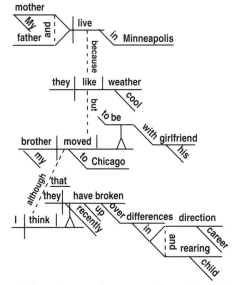

9. Royce likes to go wherever there's action.

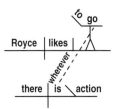

10. Having given it much thought, I decided, in the end, to stay and not worry about it.

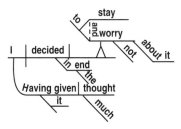

11. The account executive whom we just hired brought in three new clients.

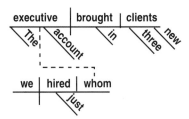

12. The book which I authored related my UFO experiences.

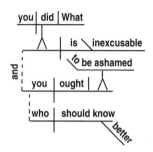

13. What you did is inexcusable, and you, who should know better, ought to be ashamed.

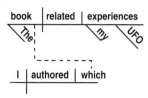

Exit/Mastery Exam, Page 65.

1. Will Bobby sing?

```
    S      P
  Bobby | Will sing
```

2. Register here.

```
    S       P
  (You) | Register
                    \ here
                       M
```

3. Cameron looked worried.

```
    S        P        PA
  Cameron | looked \ worried
```

4. He hates spinach.

```
   S     P      DO
  He | hates | spinach
```

5. The Bradfords bought a motorhome.

```
     S          P        DO
  Bradfords | bought | motorhome
```

6. Paige is on time.

```
    S    P
  Paige | is
              \ PP
            on  time
```

7. Vince ran to the store.

```
    S     P
  Vince | ran
               \ PP
             to  store
                    the
                     M
```

8. Cross the street carefully.

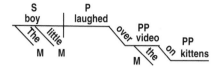

9. The little boy laughed over the video on kittens.

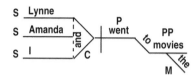

10. Lynne, Amanda, and I went to the movies.

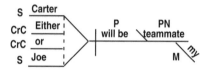

11. Either Carter or Joe will be my teammate.

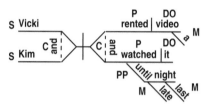

12. Vicki and Kim rented a video and watched it until late last night.

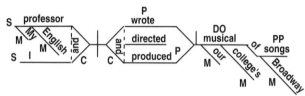

13. My English professor and I wrote, directed, and produced our college's musical of Broadway songs.

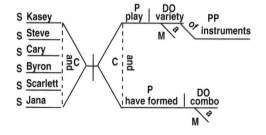

14. Kasey, Steve, Cary, Byron, Scarlett, and Jana play a variety of instruments and have formed a combo.

15. None of the gang went to the theater or rented a movie at Blockbuster video store.

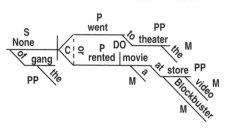

16. Don't judge him or her.

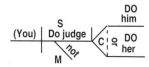

17. Will you or Barry call your parents, or write home?

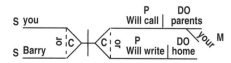

18. Rosie and Paul got married and went on a long honeymoon to the Adirondacks.

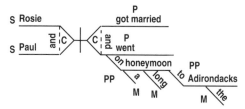

19. Is he tall, dark, and handsome?

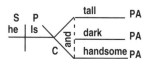

20. A girl wore wire-rim glasses, a short skirt, and spiked heels.

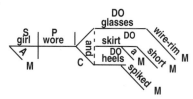

21. Two thousand or three thousand boys and girls jammed the orange and green stadium in anticipation of the rock group's appearance.

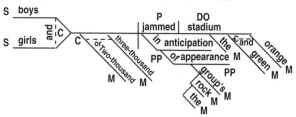

22. Shy and scared Caroline easily and correctly answered the questions on the oral and written exams for her doctoral degree.

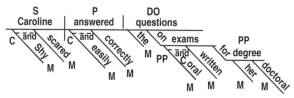

23. Disadvantaged and under-privileged cultural minorities are applying for state and federal grants.

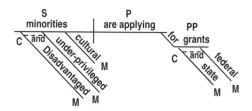

24. At the sound of the fire alarm, Cody and Yin grabbed their pants and ran outside, across the street for quick and reassuring help from neighbors.

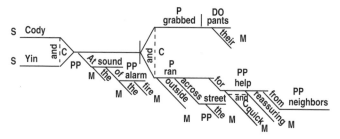

25. Claudia and Trish answered the questionnaire honestly and carefully.

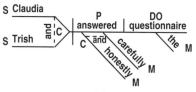

26. Annette wore navy blue and periwinkle shorts with white stripes, and a yellow top with a pattern of tiny flowers.

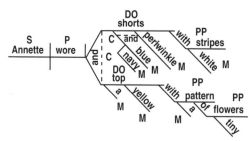

89

27. The city and county street workers tirelessly and diligently fixed old and decadent sewer covers, and damaged and chipped hydrants on Sixth Street.

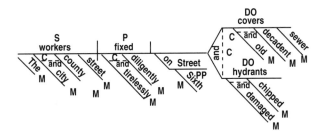

28. Hand and canister vacuum cleaners, window and free-standing fans, and Johnson and York air conditioners are on sale until the first of the month.

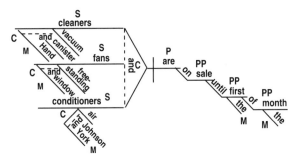

29. Boisterous, loud-mouthed, and crude Adrian is actively and obviously seeking the office of class president.

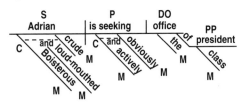

30. Dan, Mark, and Becky impatiently and nervously stood on the porch and endlessly rang the doorbell.

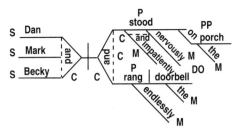

31. Dell and I washed and waxed the royal blue Toyota with yellow and blue racing stripes, and the dark green Porsche with the white sunroof.

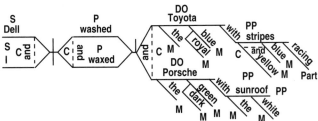

32. Tell Jill and Marnie about the books, the coupons, and the business cards.

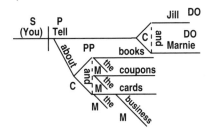

33. Send me the address and phone number for your new residence.

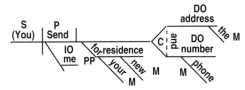

34. Nedra and Frank eagerly and excitedly picked Hillary the leader of our small but close group of writers and artists.

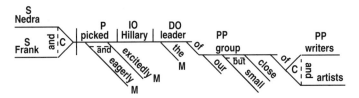

35. Can you and your colleagues reduce the pain and stress of my hectic and busy life?

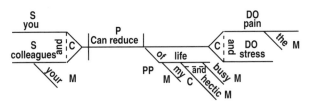

36. Kenny, Erin, and Professor Collins nominated and voted Bobby and Willy president and vice president respectively.

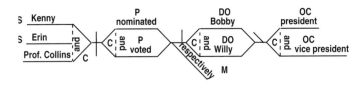

37. Little Mickey Johnson drew and colored a horse and buggy black and white.

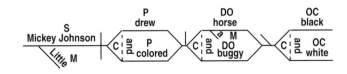

38. Did Dad and Mom name and choose Sis or Aunt Cathy executrix or power-of-attorney of their will.

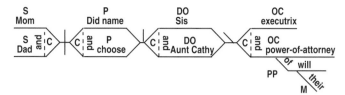

39. The high school principal and the tenth grade math teacher appointed eleventh grader Marshall, and senior Garrett, school representatives and student government delegates.

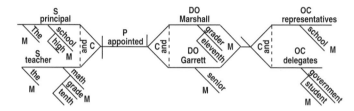

40. The county police and the county council often think Old Man Forester, the first council president, insane.

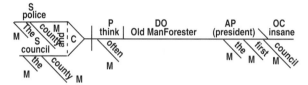

41. Ramon, Manuel, and Diego picked out and gave Sherry, Louella, and Lillian, roses, candy, and cards.

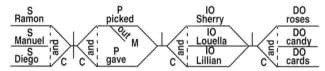

42. The prosecuting attorney, the arresting officer, and the store owner labeled the heavy-set and loud man, the little guy, and the tall woman thieves and felonious criminals.

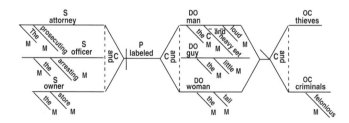

43. The President of the United States read and vetoed one bill on wetlands, but she eagerly and hurriedly passed another bill on land reclamation.

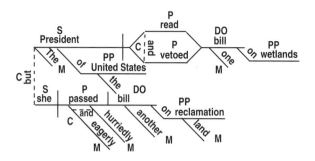

44. My cousin Reggie fervently sang the first song, and I played the violin for her.

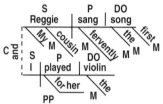

45. Today the mail was light, but tomorrow my mail box will be filled with envelopes, advertisements, and bills.

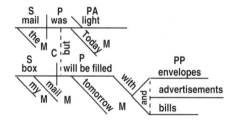

46. My Aunt Georgio lives in Niagara Falls, but she works on the Canadian side.

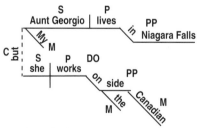

47. Exhausted and sleepy, Marty sluggishly and aimlessly rose from the bed and showered before breakfast, and then he left for work on time.

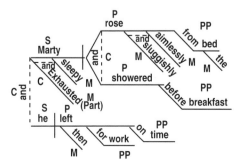

91

48. Either Earnest or Brock is going, but I don't know when.

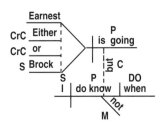

49. Cousin Lyle and his wife, Maya, live and work in Seattle, but they're from Erie originally.

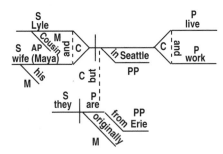

50. Gus bought a pair of red neon and orange-striped shorts, and a fancy, tailored shirt, but his brother didn't get anything.

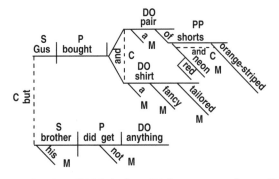

51. I applied to UCLA, but Yale accepted me first.

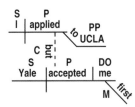

52. "Crazy" Ed admitted to the crime, but "Snake" was the perpetrator.

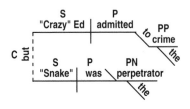

53. Are you going to guarantee the motherboard in the computer and fix the stuck key on keyboard, or will you send me an entirely new and warranted computer which should be given to me because of the aggravation I have had with this computer system?

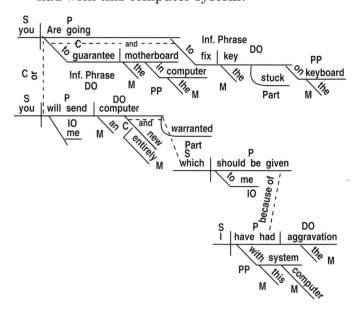

54. Roxane has to deliver the newspaper before six in the morning.

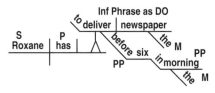

55. To forgive wholeheartedly is to love unconditionally.

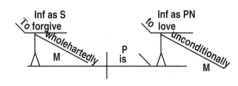

56. The gusting wind feels too powerful to walk in.

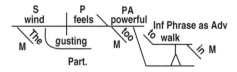

57. Madge introduced the Honorable Andrew Brady, city mayor, after Father Luke Donati gave the blessing.

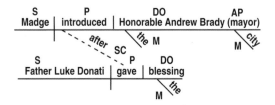

58. Jumping rope and jogging are good exercises for strengthening muscles, but you must be careful not to overdo, as damage to tendons could result, unless you do warm-ups and cool-downs.

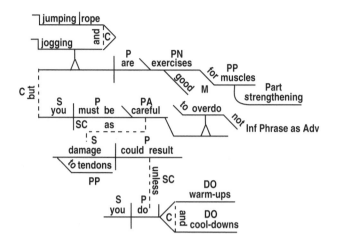

59. Although John took private and expensive driving lessons, he still flunked the driving part of the exam which many teenagers seem to fail on the first try.

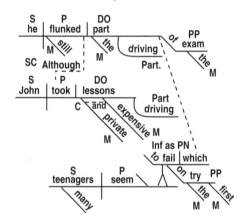

60. The minister knows that you're the cantor for next Sunday's morning sermon.

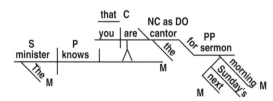

61. The novel that you finished was written by Sinclair Lewis.

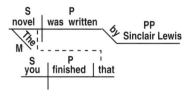

62. There's a lot to do at the new amusement park, but make sure to bring enough money unless you expect to win a bundle.

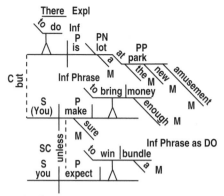

63. Honey, before you speak, think first because a wrong word uttered could upset the CEO who isn't a patient and understanding woman.

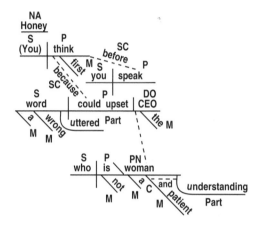

64. Gosh, sweetheart! The sunset is absolutely beautiful when the sky has a pink tinge to it.

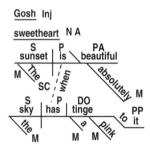

65. My son, who's a civil engineer for the city, wants to return to school for his master's degree, and then he plans on opening his own business.

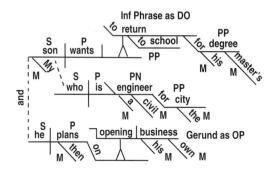

66. In researching the job market, Bentley learned that he had to better prepare by getting a college degree and relevant training.

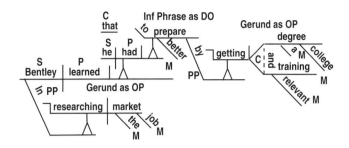

67. No, I don't want to hear about discovering a new way to get the job done.

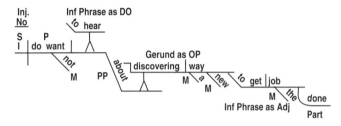

68. Look out! A train's coming and we're sitting on the tracks, and you haven't started the car's engine.

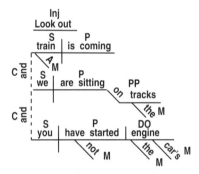

69. Wait! Don't go without me unless you're going to conduct the seminar by yourself and without the help of an expert like me.

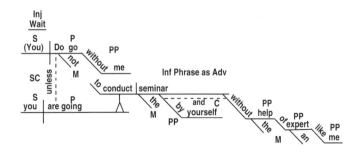

70. The building contractor, who is our old and valued friend, is going to build an 18 X 20 addition for us, but he said the roofer would put in a skylight or two.

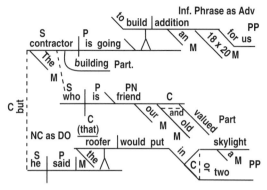

71. Heavens! Traveling by car from Maryland to Oregon is long, boring, and exhausting; but I began reading a book whenever I wasn't driving, so time passed quickly, although by having lost the directions, we were late arriving at our destination.

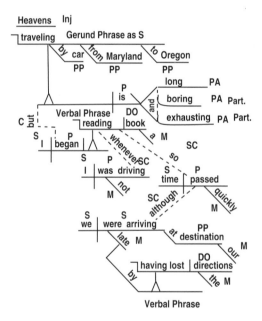

72. Yea! There's nothing to do today, which means I can leave early to do errands and buy a fancy, gold and silver bracelet for my birthday, which costs more than I want to pay.

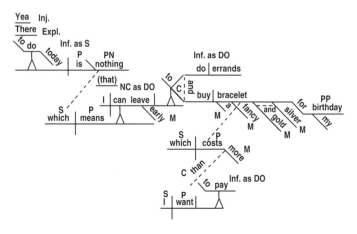

73. If you'll show me the way to Queens, I'll be able
to make my singing classes on time, providing
that your directions are clear and accurate.

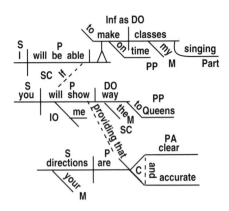

74. The play that I didn't like had a futuristic plot
to it.

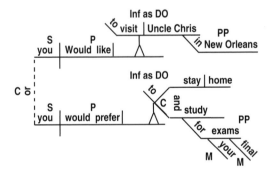

75. Would you like to visit Uncle Chris in New
Orleans, or would you prefer to stay home and
study for your final exams?

Glossary

absolute adverbs are types of adverbs that limit comparison, as in round, dead.

abstract nouns name qualities or ideas but not tangible things, such as love, greed, anger.

active voice is a property of a verb that shows that the subject does the acting instead of being acted upon.

adjective phrase includes the adjective and its modifiers that describes a noun or pronoun, whereas an **adjective clause** is a dependent clause that begins with a relative pronoun and modifies nouns and pronouns.

adjectives define or modify the meaning of a noun or pronoun; they tell what kind (**brown** eyes), which one (**that** girl), or how many (**dozen** doughnuts).

adverb is a modifier that describes verbs, adjectives, and adverbs, and often, though not always, ends in the -ly form: hurrie_dly_, anxious_ly_, eager_ly_, absolute_ly_. Adverbs tell how (walked **slowly**), where (walked **there**), when (walked **then**), and to what extent (walked **far**); although adverbs often end in an ly suffix, there are many that don't.

adverb phrase includes the adverb and its modifiers that describes a verb, adjective, or another adverb; **adverb clauses** are dependent and begin with a subordinating conjunction.

adverbial conjunctions or **conjunctive adverbs** are adverbs that connect two main clauses in a sentence; examples are: indeed, however, therefore.

appositive is a word or a group of words that rename a noun or pronoun; it appears next to the noun or pronoun and identifies or explains it.

articles are classed as adjectives and are often referred to as determiners because they determine or flag that a noun is to follow; there are various types of articles, but a few examples include a, an, the.

auxiliary verbs are helping verbs and are used with main verbs, such as *has* been, *will have* been, *could* give, and so on.

clause is a group of words placed together to form a complete thought; clauses have subjects and predicates and can be independent or dependent, but a dependent or subordinate clause cannot stand by itself.

collective nouns represent a group of the same kind of thing, place, or person, as in gaggle for a group of geese; team, class, and panel are other collective nouns.

common noun names general classes or categories, such as books, cards, homes, people.

complement is a word or group of words in a predicate that completes, renames, or describes the action of a subject, object, or verb.

complements are words or groups of words acting as nouns (predicate nominatives or predicate nouns) or as adjectives (predicate adjectives.)

complete subjects include all the words that modify (or describe) the simple subject, such as adjectives and other modifiers.

complex sentences have one independent clause, and at least one subordinate clause and is joined by a conjunction: The boy became angry *when* his classmate hit him. The subordinating conjunction *when* joins the two clauses.

compound personal pronouns or **reflexive and intensive pronouns**: See reflexive pronouns.

compound predicate consists of two or more verbs in a sentence.

compound sentences have two or more independent or main clauses joined by a conjunction but act as one unit; they have no subordinate (or dependent) clause: I went clothes shopping *but* I didn't buy anything. The coordinating conjunction *but* joins the two main clauses.

compound subject consists of more than one noun or groups of words being talked about by the predicate.

compound-complex sentences have two or more independent clauses, and at least one dependent or subordinate clause, and are joined by conjunctions: The garage that Roman had built had only one bay, so he added a second one. The conjunctions *that* and *so* join the phrase and clause to the main sentence.

concrete nouns name tangible things: book, coat, horse.

conjunctions are parts of speech that join or link related sentence components. They are connectors or words that join one part of a sentence to another; these include coordinating conjunctions (yet, so), correlative conjunctions (either . . . or), and subordinating conjunctions (although, because).

conjunctive adverbs or **adverbial conjunctions** are types of adverbs that connect independent clauses; these include however, indeed, therefore.

contractions are abbreviations of an expression and usually contain an apostrophe to substitute for the missing letters, as in wasn't for was not or couldn't for could not.

coordinating conjunctions are seven grammatical structures that link or join like or equivalent parts of a sentence: but, so, for, now, and, or, and yet.

correlative conjunctions are pairs of words that work together to connect equivalent sentence parts; there are five pairs: either . . . or; neither . . . nor; both . . . and; not only . . . but also; whether . . . or.

declarative sentences make or affirm a statement or fact, and are followed by a period: Edgar Allan Poe died in Baltimore.

demonstrative pronouns refer to distance or nearness, and point out people and objects; they include this, that, these, those.

diagramming is a graphic or visual representation showing how one part of a sentence relates to another.

direct address is a grammatical construction in which a word or phrase indicates the person or group spoken to, and is set off by a comma or commas, such as in, The weather, *Barbara,* doesn't permit sled riding. See Nouns of Address.

direct object (DO) is a noun, pronoun, or any word acting as a noun that receives the action of a transitive verb or verb form, and thus completes the meaning of the sentence. In "We watched television," the word *television* is the direct object.

exclamatory sentences express strong feelings or emphasize a point, and are usually followed by exclamation points; these are often interjections: "I said no**!**"

expletive is a sentence construction beginning with the word *it* or the word *there* and is followed by the verb form *to be* as in "*It* is time that we go."

fragment is a part of a sentence only; either the subject or the predicate is missing.

fused sentence has two main clauses joined together without proper punctuation; also known as a run-on sentence.

gerunds are verbals that end in the *-ing* form and function as nouns, such as *Skiing* is a fun but dangerous sport.

imperative mood is a verb mood that gives commands, such as Stop!

imperative sentences command or tell, or order someone to do something, and may be followed by a period: "Wait for the bus."

incomplete sentence may also be called a fragment, as no complete thought is conveyed since either the subject or the predicate is missing.

indefinite pronouns don't refer to a particular or "definite" person or thing, and include such singular and plural (or both) pronouns as anything, everybody, many, most, and so on.

independent clause is a main grammatical unit with a subject and a predicate, that can stand alone as a sentence.

indicative mood is the most common mood for verbs because it makes a statement about real things, or things likely to happen, or it asks questions about facts or statements; an example is "John will come tomorrow."

indirect objects (IO) are verb complements that are nouns or pronouns and answer the questions for whom or to whom or for what and to what.

infinitives are the plain forms of verbs (as seen in dictionaries) that are often coupled with the word *to,* and may act as verbals in the form of an adjective, adverb, or noun.

intensive and **reflexive pronouns** or **compound personal pronouns**: See reflexive pronouns.

interjections express powerful emotions such as hate, disgust, happiness, grief, surprise, and thus are followed by an exclamation mark: Ugh! Of course! Hurry! Look out! Help! Now!, and so on. They are words that stand by themselves or are inserted into a thought, and command attention.

interrogative mood asks a question.

interrogative sentences ask questions; followed by a question mark: Are we there yet**?**

intransitive verbs do not take direct objects, nor are they linking verbs.

irregular verbs are those verbs whose endings are formed or conjugated in some way other than by adding *-d* or *-ed.*

linking verbs are a type of verb or predicate that connects or links the subject to its complement; the verb form *to be* is often linking, as are verbs that make up the five senses.

mode is a verb characteristic that expresses emotions, feelings, or ideas.

modifiers are words or group of words that describe or limit other words; these include adverbs and adjectives, and those phrases and clauses that behave like adverbs and adjectives.

modify means to describe or qualify something,

mood refers to how the verb conveys the writer's attitude about the action he or she is expressing. The English language relies on three moods: imperative, indicative, and subjunctive.

nonrestrictive appositive is a word or group of words that renames the noun, and is set off by commas or dashes, as in "A 1985 Corvette, a red one, is the first car I've ever owned."

noun complement is another name for predicate noun or predicate nominative.

nouns are a part of speech that names persons, places, or things; may perform in different ways, such as sentence subjects, objects, and so on; may be proper or common.

nouns of address name or address a person, place, or thing, such as *"Bob,* will you please come here."

number is a verb property or characteristic that represents the number of those speaking or acting in a sentence.

object complements (OC) may be nouns or adjectives, as in "Elect Joe president," where the noun *president* complements the direct object *Joe.* The subject of the sentence is *you* and is understood to be in the sentence.

object of a preposition (OP) is a noun, or pronoun, or those words acting as nouns or pronouns that complete the meaning of a preposition. In the prepositional phrase "by Monday morning," the word *morning* is the object of the preposition *by.* The word *Monday* acts as a modifier.

object pronouns are pronouns or words that act as nouns that perform as the object of a sentence, and include me, you, him, her, it, us, them.

objects are nouns, pronouns, or a group of words that behave as nouns or pronouns that receive the action of a verb. Direct objects, indirect objects, and objects of prepositions are examples of objects.

part of speech is a name for any one of the eight classes or categories that words are grouped into based on form, function, and meaning.

participial phrases are verbal phrases acting as adjectives that contain the present or past participle and all its modifiers.

participles are verbals that show action but are used as adjectives, and never serve as a sentence's predicate; examples include *used* cars, *riding* boots. Participles may appear in the present or past tense, and may have several words combined with them to form phrases or clauses.

passive voice is a property of a verb that shows that the subject has been acted upon instead of doing the action.

person represents from whose viewpoint a story or an account is being told; there are three major forms of person: First person *(I),* second person *(you),* third person *(he, she, it).*

personal pronouns: See subject pronouns.

phrase is a group of words that lacks either a subject or a predicate, or both, and thus does not contain a complete thought. There are a number of different types of phrases, such as prepositional phrases and verbal phrases.

plural refers to more than one person or thing experiencing an action, and thus takes a plural verb in order to be in subject-verb agreement.

plural nouns represent more than one kind of thing, place, or person, such as people for person.

possessive nouns show ownership, as in *Barb's* dog, indicating that the dog belongs to Barb.

possessive pronouns show ownership, such as my, mine, ours, their, your.

predicate adjectives (PA) are adjectives that complement or complete the subject, and follow a linking verb, as in "Candy is sweet," where *sweet* refers to the subject *candy*.

predicate noun or **predicate nominative (PN)** is a noun complement or subject complement that follows a linking verb and modifies or refers to the subject, such as "He is the king," where the word *king* refers to *he* and thus is a predicate noun or nominative.

preposition is a word that serves as a link for a noun or words acting like nouns. They relate a noun or pronoun to some other word in a sentence; they also introduce phrases, and they may be singular or compound: of, on, under, over, to.

principal clause is the main or independent clause.

pronoun is a word that substitutes for a noun; there are different types of pronouns, such as personal and relative pronouns. Pronouns name persons, places, or things; examples: he, she, they.

proper adjectives describe or qualify, and are called proper because they derive from proper nouns. Italian marble, and Shakespearean play, are two examples.

proper noun names a specific thing, place, or person, such as the title of someone, as in Mr. Cummings.

prepositional phrase is comprised of the preposition and its object with all its modifiers; these kinds of phrases behave as adjectives or adverbs.

reflexive and intensive pronouns, or **compound personal pronouns** end in *-self* or *-selves* as they reflect on or refer to the sentence's subject, thus making the sentence and the object the same: ourselves, itself, myself. They're called "intensive" because they intensify the meaning of a sentence since they reflect on the sentence's subject.

regular verbs refer to the majority of verbs in the English language; these are verbs that form their past tense and present participle by adding ed or d to its simple or infinitive form. See Irregular Verbs for comparison.

relative pronouns or **interrogative pronouns** ask a question and include who, which, that.

restrictive appositives are words or a group of words that rename the noun, and are **not** set off by a comma or commas, as in "My brother *John* lives a thousand miles from me."

run-on sentence is the same as a fused sentence, in which punctuation is lacking, and two main clauses are run together as one thought.

sentence predicate is the action part of the sentence that contains a finite verb.

sentence subject is the noun or group of words being talked about in the predicate.

simple predicate is the key action verb in the sentence, without its modifiers.

simple sentences have only one main (or independent) clause: Dogs are lovable animals.

simple subjects contain only the key word of a sentence which is usually a noun or pronoun or a verbal.

singular refers to only one person or thing experiencing an action, and thus takes a singular verb in order to be in subject-verb agreement.

subject complement (SC) is a word or group of words that complete or complement the subject, as in predicate nominatives or predicate nouns.

subject pronouns are pronouns or words that represent nouns that act as the subject of a sentence; they include I, you, he, she, it, we, they. These are also called **personal pronouns**.

subject-verb agreement refers to a singular subject taking a singular verb, and a plural subject taking a plural verb; it is the match between the subject and the verb in number.

subjunctive mood expresses wishes, speculations, or requests, as in "I wish she were here."

subordinate clauses are dependent clauses or those that cannot stand alone, and is introduced by **subordinating conjunctions**.

subordinating conjunctions introduce adverbial clauses, and link or show how they're related to the independent clause. Examples are after, because, as if, while.

tense expresses the time at which a verb's action happens (past, present, future); it may include helping verbs, as well as reflect a verb's inflection. Depicting the various verb forms is referred to as conjugation.

transitive verbs convey action and do take objects.

verb complements include direct objects and indirect objects.

verb is the action part of the sentence or the do-er of the sentence that indicates the state of the subject of the sentence. Verbs tell what the person, place, or thing is doing in a sentence, and they may be action or nonaction (passive) in nature. In the sentence, "John dashes down the street," the word *dashes* is the verb or predicate.

verb phrase acts as a verb in a sentence, and includes the main verb and any helping verbs.

verbals are parts of verbs that function as nouns, adjectives, or adverbs; there are three main types of verbals: infinitives, participles, gerunds. Verbals may have subjects, objects, complements, and modifiers.

voice: Verbs can have active or passive voice. While transitive verbs are usually active, intransitive (linking) verbs make the voice passive. See **active** and **passive** voice.